# THE OTHER HALF

## Glimpses of Grassroots Asia

# THE OTHER HALF

## Glimpses of Grassroots Asia

*Peter C. Stuart*

F A R     H O R I Z O N     B O O K S

Far Horizon Books
Box 10
Alton, Illinois 62002

Library of Congress Catalog Card Number: 89-83723

ISBN 0-9622350-4-0

Cover photograph: washing clothes in a stream near Paete, Laguna province, Philippines (by the author).
Cover design and graphic by Melissa Olson
Book design by Vivian L. Bradbury
Composition by Sans Serif Inc., Ann Arbor, Michigan 48104
Printed by McNaughton & Gunn, Saline, Michigan 48176

*For my wife, Vicky*

# CONTENTS

This book gives the interested reader a valuable update. As they go into the last 10 years of the 20th century, scientific farming has enabled most Asians to grow enough food (India and China doing well, the Indonesians doubling rice production by 1985 to an amazing 26 million tons).

But the Pill and IUD seem sadly outdistanced still by antibiotics. The postcolonial expansion of primary education has been too slow. Women are still badly neglected. And the staggeringly big urban populations, as villagers keep swarming into cities, are way beyond our historical experience. I was particularly alarmed by Peter Stuart's account of how heavily so many people have come to rely on oil, since oil prices seem certain to soar again in the mid-1990's.

Mr. Stuart, formerly with *The Christian Science Monitor*'s Washington bureau and for four years a much-travelled officer of the Asian Development Bank, is an honest, trustworthy, and sensitive reporter.

For most of us, busy with our own lives, "the other half" of the human race too easily slips out of sight and out of mind. *The Other Half* is a reminder that Asia's ancient civilizations are desperately adapting to our most advanced scientific techniques, and on their success or failure to curb population growth and find better lives through scientific farming, electronics, new energy sources, and other advances, lies our future too. It is highly recommended.

—Richard Critchfield,
author of the acclaimed book *Villages*

# Introduction
# The Media's Uncovered Majority

A visiting American journalist had just arrived in Manila.

The swarms of children along his route from the airport are the product of the highest birthrate in Southeast Asia.

The urchins who tapped grimy fingers on the window of his taxi, begging for pesos, are among the four out of five Philippine children who are malnourished.

The tumbledown shacks visible up the side-streets, if he was watching, house some of the 40 per cent of the population living below poverty level.

The youths loitering in the parking lot of his hotel are part of the one-third of the labor force without jobs.

The visitor's first question to his local host: "How's Marcos' health?"

\* \* \*

Seven years ago, I drew the cover over my typewriter for the last time, boxed up my notebooks, and walked out of the Washington bureau of *The Christian Science Monitor* — and out of journalism.

Seventeen years in the business of informing people about what was going on around them, practiced from Midwestern city halls to the U.S. Capitol and overseas, had left me with a troubling conviction: that Americans weren't getting from their news media a very valid view of the world.

The world — humankind — was seriously under-covered, I came to believe. And what coverage there was, I was persuaded by my years of increasingly skeptical political reportage, was unjustifiably political in nature.

My disenchantment drove me halfway around the world to a job as information officer of the Asian Development Bank, a multilateral lending institution of 47 member countries, based in Manila.

Four years spent outside journalism — living and travelling widely in the

1

world's most populous continent as an international civil servant — only confirmed the conclusions reached while inside the profession.

Third World government officials frequently complain that the Western news-gathering network is too pervasive. It may look that way to them. But judged from the standpoint of adequately informing its Western audience, the network is far too skimpy.

For every correspondent posted abroad by the four major Western news agencies (Associated Press, United Press International, Reuters, and Agence France Presse, taken together), there are four reporting in the home country.[1] The American newspaper with the most correspondents covering the world (*The New York Times*, with about 30)[2] has more than that covering Washington. The largest newspaper chain in the United States (Gannett) maintains not a single foreign correspondent.[3]

The trend is going Gannett's way. The number of American journalists of all kinds serving abroad (as registered by the Overseas Press Club) has shrunk from well over 500 in 1969 to barely 400 today.[4]

Where is this dwindling band of correspondents positioned in order to inform the West about the rest of the world? Over half of the Americans are based in Europe.[5] The American wire services AP and UPI are reckoned to have more correspondents in their London offices than in all of Africa. And the European agencies Reuters and AFP, which are preeminent in Africa, have more staffers in the United States.[6]

What often passes in the United States for coverage of the world is coverage of the Department of State. Scores of publications which never entertained the notion of assigning a reporter abroad, assign one to Foggy Bottom. He or she attends the daily briefings, cultivates a few "country desk" officers, and maybe joins the press party accompanying the Secretary of State on an overseas trip — flashing home to readers the official communiqués and exchanges of banquet toasts. The man or woman at State becomes known as the publication's "foreign affairs writer."

There's nothing wrong about covering the State Department. It ought to be covered. But there's plenty wrong about rating it as a suitable substitute for on-the-spot coverage of the world. Not only is such reportage hopelessly far-removed and second-hand, but it reflects (let us never forget) the American government's view of the world. What self-respecting newspaper would "cover" its city or state by sending a reporter only to elicit the official views at City Hall or the statehouse?

The weight given to diplomatic coverage of the world is, in the end, only part of a larger distortion in the way journalism informs humanity about itself: a preoccupation with governments and rulers.

A recent study of what sort of news about the Third World is transmitted by the four major wire services confirms what any perceptive reader might have suspected—most of it has to do with governance. News about foreign relations, domestic politics, and military and political violence makes up over half (55.6 per cent) of their daily output.[7]

No bilateral tiff, state visit, or cabinet reshuffle, it seems, escapes dutiful—and frequently lavish—reporting. Judging by the news, just about all of consequence that goes on in the rest of the world are the affairs of monarchs, presidents, premiers, and assorted politicians. Instead of coverage of China, we get coverage of Deng Xiaoping; instead of coverage of India, of Rajiv Gandhi.

(The Third World's own news media are often just as transfixed by the doings of their leaders. The summit meeting of non-aligned countries in 1983 in New Delhi may have been the most heavily-covered event in the history of Third World journalism—attracting more than 1,000 reporters—although it is questionable whether the meeting materially affected the life of a single person anywhere in the world.)

Often the only time a foreign land becomes "newsworthy" is when its leader does something to make it so. The ritual inaugurations of Philippine President Ferdinand E. Marcos for another predetermined term of office, and the recent meeting between Indonesian President Suharto and U.S. President Ronald Reagan in Bali—non-events, if ever there were any—generated the standard "situationers" that only emphasized the dearth of meaningful reportage on these countries the rest of the time.

It would be hard to find a scrap of evidence that the palace-and-politics occurrences which are the journalistic staple have much real relevance in the countries involved.

My own observation is that in rural Asia, where upwards of two-thirds of the people live, life grinds along as before, largely unaffected by—and often unaware of—even the most momentous political events in the distant capital. After all, most Asians (like most others in the Third World) are subsistence farmers, eking out a living in a manner that has changed little through the centuries while kingdoms and potentates have come and gone.

Thailand's old Prince Sithiporn, from a perspective gained after 87 years in the labyrinthine world of his country's royal court, got it about right. He averred that the poor rice farmer was more important than any amount of royal intrigue—and was jailed for such heresy.[8]

Even Mao Zedong, whose revolution probably rippled farther than most, confessed to President Richard Nixon in a moment of candor: "I have only been able to change a few places in the vicinity of Peking."[9]

Gunnar Myrdal, the Nobel laureate and author of the classic socioeconomic study *Asian Drama*, has written that "changes of government, or even of form of government, occur high above the heads of the masses of people and mainly imply merely a shift of the groups of persons in the upper strata who monopolize power."[10]

If such news-events are so little important to so many people, isn't there something wrong with a concept of news that misallocates so much journalistic resources to cover them?

The reasons for it—if not the justifications—are understandable enough. It's easier, of course, and more cost-effective to cover the rulers than the masses. Covering Deng Xiaoping is a cinch compared with covering 1 billion Chinese.

Reared journalistically on a diet of covering mayors, governors, parliaments, and presidents, Western newsmen on assignment overseas tend, by sheer force of habit, to sniff out the political side of things. It's also more ego-gratifying. Most reporters, given a choice, would rather hob-nob with a prime minister than discuss rice yields with a lowly peasant.

Serious news-stories lacking a politico-military angle, no matter how significant they may be, tend to be regarded by correspondents as dull—both for them and for their public. Such a view may spring from unfamiliarity. True, these stories may take a little more enterprise and imagination, but all the raw materials are there for strong reportage with audience appeal.

One story barely covered in the West (unless I've missed it) is the remarkable march toward self-sufficiency in food by two of the world's largest countries and, until recently, largest food importers—India and Indonesia, which together encompass a quarter of humanity.

Other stories lie in the abysmal under-use of female resources in the Third World, and the resulting drag on development and population control; the reliance of many Third World nations on the oil-rich Middle East for exporting surplus labor and propping up their frail economies with the money that overseas workers send home; the life-transforming impact of the steady trickle of "city" amenities into the rural villages where most people in the world still live.

But perhaps the most important story that the press is failing to communicate—if it can be called a story as such—is the enormous wealth and comfort enjoyed by the tiny minority of people fortunate enough to live in the industrialized countries, compared to the rest of their fellow humans.

The average working American, for example, earns as much money in one week as the average Asian makes in a year. A similar chasm separates their living conditions. The "basic necessities" taken for granted in the West, such as clean running water and electricity, are undreamed-of luxuries most everywhere else. We're the world's rich elite, and in sharing the place with so many more who are so much less favored, it would seem best never to be allowed to forget it.

After the hard lessons of Vietnam and Iran—which demonstrated how poorly the media had informed Americans about those societies—it should be unnecessary to suggest the perils of continuing to cover the world through journalism-as-usual.

Doing a better job isn't so much a question of resources as of will. The industrialized countries, as the "haves" of this world, alone possess the capability to inform themselves about the rest of the globe. They have the human, technological, and financial wherewithal. Look what they can do with an assassination or a summit meeting. Aren't the stakes high enough to begin using this capability more responsibly?

\* \* \*

Here, then, are glimpses of that majority of humanity largely uncovered by the media—the Asians who make up more than half of the earth's population.

The people who amble through the following pages are "ordinary" folk. There are among them no presidents or generals, guerrilla leaders or terrorists, tycoons or gurus.

But the struggles, aspirations, and occasional triumphs of these common people—multiplied by millions upon millions of Asians sharing much the same sort of lives—are every bit as newsworthy as the actions of the lofty or outrageous few who attract the headlines.

And these everyday concerns are immeasurably more useful in cultivating a better understanding of a world in which most of us are just such Asians.

The people whom the reader is about to meet—and they are all real people—are introduced to illustrate significant aspects of Asian life. The chapters in which they appear are grouped according to the types of day-by-day challenges confronting them. The emphasis throughout falls on the ongoing efforts, mostly humble, occasionally grand, to cope with these challenges.

The Asians in these pages are drawn from just about every corner of the region, with two very large exceptions: China and India. The omission occurs simply because I have done no interviewing in these two countries.

But both nations have been visited and incorporated into the discussions, for conditions there broadly reflect those prevailing elsewhere in Asia.

It is my earnest hope that the encounter with these few grassroots Asians, seemingly so very different and distant, may leave the reader with a more generous appreciation of their world—and of his own.

# Making Enough Money to Live

RASAU KERTEH, MALAYSIA

Slipping off his shoes at the bottom step with as much respect as if he were entering a sultan's palace, Harun Mamat pads barefoot up a set of open wooden steps and plops down on a bench on the tiny porch of his house.

The place is a one-story, unpainted timber-plank house with a steeply-pitched roof, perched chest-high above the ground on posts. Inside are a few pieces of simple furniture and one obviously-prized cabinet with a swatch of white lace on top. The bare corrugated-steel roof forms the ceiling.

Not much, perhaps, but to this young father of three it's something of a dream house. Having owned little more than the clothes on his back for most of his life, he now owns his own home.

The master of the house is a lithe 29-year-old with a face scoured smooth by outdoor labor in a climate rather like a steam laundry. The hair has been beaten into retreat above a broad, brown forehead. He wears pink jeans and a tee-shirt with Arabic script stencilled across the front.

Relaxing after a day's work in a nearby oil-palm plantation, the little porch affords a breezy refuge from the blistering late-afternoon sun.

As Harun squints out across his front yard, flowering bushes clinging to the sand, he recalls the harsher life he led just a few years ago as a fisherman in a coastal village 25 miles from here on the South China Sea.

The fishing village he left behind is one of those, dotting the coast, that the occasional tourists who venture here find so photogenic. It is. Salt-bleached wooden huts, tottering on stilts, are strewn like driftwood beneath towering coconut palms leaning gracefully over a shimmering beach worthy of Club Med.

But the prettiness masks economic hardship. Tossing on a fickle sea every day from dawn until dark, in obsolete and ill-equipped boats owned by others, village fishermen earn the equivalent of $75 a month—well below the poverty line.

"Your income fluctuates," says Harun in soft-toned Malay through an interpreter, "and you own nothing."

One day he heard about a series of five new towns being carved out of the jungle in Trengganu, a state on the eastern coast of peninsular Malaysia which ranks as one of the country's least developed.

Forsaking his all-too-often empty fishing nets, he moved to Rasau Kerteh and was introduced to the oil palm. This stout, feathery-fronded palm is the soybean of tropical Asia. Its volleyball-sized clusters of reddish fruit are processed into vegetable oil, soap, and other household products.

In a more egalitarian version of the old colonial plantation system, Harun and 23 other new-town residents each were given ownership of adjoining 10-acre plots of an oil-palm estate, which they tend communally.

The jump in his income—to between $500 and $650 a month—is helping to finance his house. After three years as a renter, he exercised the option to begin buying it. The cost of homeownership: about $900.

With it come such amenities as safe running water, sewage disposal, electricity, schools, shops, and the customary Asian market of small fruit and vegetable stalls.

Many residents, as their standard of living rises, are adding other amenities of their own. Some are building new rooms, brushing on a coat of paint, or otherwise individualizing their rudimentary houses. Others, like Harun, have bought Honda motorbikes.

And one of his boyhood chums, another ex-fisherman named Tuan Dalam Bin Tuanbesar, is even buying, on credit, that worldwide symbol of comfortable living: a television set.

Most of the settlers, as in the case of Harun, are poor migrants from other parts of Trengganu and Kelantan, an adjoining state that borders Thailand on the north. And they are mainly Malays, the country's most disadvantaged racial group. While settlers originally had to be coaxed to come, the waiting list of applicants has now swollen to 20,000.

* * *

Although Harun and his thousands of newly-propertied neighbors are aware of it only dimly, if at all, they are numbered among a favored and much-envied minority in the developing world. They are escapees. They have been sprung from the trap of poverty which continues to grip hundreds of millions of others.

The Third World has no corner, of course, on poverty. It exists everywhere. The great difference lies in its extent and severity. In the West, most people live comfortably, although there are pockets of poverty. In the developing world, most people live in poverty, with pockets of affluence.

Worldwide, a majority of the more than 4 billion humans are classified by the United Nations Commission on Human Rights as poor—that is, unable to meet their basic needs. An estimated 850 million of them exist in circumstances of extreme want—described by the World Bank as "a condition of life so characterized by malnutrition, illiteracy, and disease as to be beneath any reasonable definition of human decency."[1]

Three-quarters of the world's poor live in Asia. These 750 millions, as tabulated by the World Bank, constitute most of the population of the continent's developing nations (57 per cent). In country after country—China, India (which between them contain nearly half of mankind), Indonesia, Bangladesh, Pakistan, Philippines, Burma, Nepal—from 40 per cent to as much as 85 per cent of the populace qualify as destitute.

In financial terms, an average Asian lives on about one-fortieth as much annual income (about $375) as the average American ($15,450 in 1984).[2]

And many of those in the West categorized as poor—with their cars, color television sets, food stamps, and monthly welfare checks—would be regarded by Asians as downright rich. The U.S. government's official poverty line of $10,609 for a family of four (or about $5,200 for one person, as designated in 1984) represents dreamy wealth for most Asians.

The poverty line in the Philippines, by contrast, is a rock-bottom $200 a year per person; in India, Indonesia, and Thailand, it's around $100. And welfare assistance is practically unknown.

The legal minimum wage in the United States, similarly, far exceeds the maximum earnings that most Asians, in their wildest imaginations, might ever hope to rake in.

The lowest allowable American wage of $3.35 per hour[3] compares with an equivalent of 13 cents per hour in Bangladesh, for example, or 9 cents per hour in Sri Lanka. Thus a Bangladeshi being paid the minimum wage must work more than three days to earn as much as an American paid on the same basis collects in just one hour. A Sri Lankan must work four and a half days to do so.

Liberal exemptions and lax enforcement, moreover, leave vast numbers of Asian workers receiving less than even the paltry official minimum wage.

Comprising, as they do, a majority of the Asian population—spanning a rich diversity of countries, cultures, and tongues—Asia's poor are a varied lot. But there are enough similarities to draw a sketchy composite portrait.

The average poor Asian:
- Spends as much as four-fifths of his meager income for food, consisting largely of rice or other foodgrains with a bit of fish, meat, or vegetables.[4] Yet he (or she) is likely to be undernourished, consuming fewer than the minimum daily requirement of calories.[5]
- Devotes several hours every day or so to scrounging for wood for the family's cooking fire—a chore entailing increasingly longer treks and time as Asia's forests are systematically stripped away.[6]
- Hauls the family's water, by hand or atop the head, over some distance from a communal spigot, stream, pond, or other source of dubious quality.
- Walks wherever he's going. The only ride he's ever likely to get is on the back of a plodding water buffalo or in a swaying bullock cart. An automobile? Few Asians ever see one. Only one of every 785 Indians has a car, one of every 2,000 Bangladeshis, one of every 10,000 Chinese.[7]
- Lives in a hut of straw, mud, or scrap lumber without electricity, a toilet, a telephone, more than a few sticks of furniture, or even window-screens to keep out the clouds of insects.
- Is likely—and, if a woman, very likely—to be illiterate, unable to fathom a sign or read a newspaper.[8]
- Lacks regular access to a doctor, despite the flourishing of poverty-related diseases, as well as others such as malaria and leprosy which Westerners often presume to have gone the way of the Black Plague.[9]
- Can expect to live less than 60 years.[10]

Hundreds of millions of Asians find themselves in these conditions through no personal negligence. They have not lazed, overspent, or bungled themselves into poverty. They simply had the misfortune to be born into a part of the world cursed with too many people, too punishing a climate, too few resources, and too late an entry into the modern age.

Chances are, they are eking out a subsistence from the same reluctant patch of sea, tired rice paddy, or squalid city streets as their parents and grandparents did before them—and as their children seem condemned to do after them.

A fortunate few are being extricated. It can happen in various ways: the sudden smiling of world market forces, a providential "lucky break," or (as in Harun's case) the coming of a foreign-aid project.

Springing out often seems to require, as well, a certain receptivity on the part of the person involved—a readiness to make a clean break with the familiar.

Leaving a life of grinding poverty might seem to be something no one would resist. But among Asia's poor, most of whom live in rural areas, customs and traditions run deep, and knowledge of the world may reach little beyond one's own village. This is hardly a recipe for much social fluidity. And, with opportunities so few, perhaps it's just as well.

\* \* \*

Another who got out is Mohammed Eunus, a tossle-haired slip of a lad living in Bangladesh, one of the world's poorest countries.

Mohammed affects a maturity beyond his years, striking erect postures and setting his jaw sternly. But he is betrayed by the boyish softness in his eyes, and by the way his yellow shirt and plaid, ankle-length sarong (called a *lungi* here) drape baggily from his slight frame.

He was one of six children on a tiny family farm. His future as a farmer looked bleak. Under the Islamic law of inheritance in this strictly Islamic country, that farm—already uneconomically small—would one day be divided among all six children.

Mohammed left home. Fibbing about his age—he's probably younger than the 17 he claims to be—he landed a job on a rubber plantation north of Chittagong.

Stands of rubber trees, like those in which Mohammed works, are among the most evocative features of the Asian agricultural landscape. Long rows of slender trunks in mottled grey, supporting a leafy green canopy gently filtering the sunlight, they bespeak shade, serenity, and order in a torrid and teeming land.

But at dawn, when the plantation workers first set bleary eyes upon them, the rubber trees can look far less hospitable. Mist-enshrouded, cold, and rather ghostly, the groves are invaded every morning by "tappers" such as Mohammed.

Guiding a small knife—careful to avoid wounding the tree by cutting too deep—the tapper slices away a thin strip of bark to release a dribble of milky latex.

Mohammed finds the unfamiliar work hard, but says he likes it. What he likes most, however, is making enough money for a decent living.

Except for his age, Mohammed is typical of the roughly 1,000 tappers working on this plantation. Most are drawn from impoverished local family farms.

His supervisor, Mohammed Montaz Ali, a serious-faced young man of 30, was prodded from his father's farm by the sharp realization that, with four brothers, there wasn't enough acreage to go around.

"There was little room for survival," he explains in Bengali. "Here I have better prospects."

Here he also has some of the simple luxuries that might have remained beyond his reach as a subsistence-level farmer: his own radio, and, in the tappers' clubhouse, a television set.

It's a privileged taste of a regrettably rare phenomenon upward mobility among Asia's downtrodden.

# BATURAJA, INDONESIA

The train is an oven on wheels, grinding its way fitfully through the steamy Sumatra jungle.

Metal shutters, cranked down over the windows of the passenger coach, keep the sun out—but the heat in. Four ceiling fans slowly churn the warmth.

The occasional raising of a shutter reveals mile after searing mile of densely-tangled trees, vines, and underbrush, broken by languid, cocoa-colored rivers.

Here and there a crude field has been hacked from the jungle. A reed hut perches on stilts in the middle, surrounded by floppy-leaved banana plants whose fruits can be hawked for a few rupiahs to train passengers at the next little country station down the line.

It is from harsh, hand-to-mouth rural conditions such as these that Suma-trans are fleeing to the relative allure of cities that daily grow more overcrowded.

So it is throughout the world's largest continent.

The population of Asian cities is forecast by the United Nations Economic and Social Commission for Asia and the Pacific (ESCAP) to double by the year 2000.[1]

That's an increase of nearly 700 million—the equivalent of 100 New York Cities.

Urbanization is a rather recent occurrence in Asia. Life here has been rooted in rural villages since the dawning of civilization, and still largely is.

Barely one Asian in four (about 27 per cent) lives in a city.[2] The steep increase projected by the turn of the century will still leave three-fifths of the populace in the countryside. But the continent will be significantly less rural.

As recently as 1950, there were only two Asian cities containing 5 million or more people—Tokyo and Shanghai.

By the arrival of the 21st century, there are expected to be 25 that large. And 14 of them will comprise almost half of the world's 30 biggest cities, each with a population exceeding 10 million.[3]

Because this urban population boom is occurring in societies so poverty-stricken, the problems dwarf anything faced by American and European cities when they underwent their rapid growth decades ago.

Slums and squatter settlements house nearly four out of every 10 Asian city-dwellers (an estimated 37 per cent).[4]

In Bombay, India's richest city, over a third of the people live in rowhouse tenements called *chawls* and shantytowns called *bustees*. That's a slum population the size of Los Angeles—roughly 3 million.[5]

In Manila, 2 million occupy makeshift squatter colonies.[6] In Jakarta, a third of the housing is classified as temporary.[7] In Karachi, whose work force grows by 100,000 every month, 2 million of the 5 million residents reside in what are known as *katchi adabis*, or illegal settlements.[8]

Far from improving, such conditions are expected to get worse. By the year 2000, two-thirds of the people in Asian cities are predicted to be living in slums.[9]

The population surge in the continent's cities is fueled not by procreation but migration.

Virtually everywhere, there is a drifting out of the villages into the cities. And virtually everywhere, countries are trying, however feebly, to stem it.

Indonesia has declared Jakarta and certain other places "closed" cities, where migrants are denied access to some types of jobs, housing, and education. India has resettled migrants back in the countryside. South Korea, where 70 per cent of urban growth over the past two decades has come from the rural influx, subsidizes the moving costs of those who wish to leave its largest cities.

On the more coercive side, China forcibly relocated 10 million to 15 million urban high-school graduates into rural areas between 1969 and 1973.

Only the Chinese authorities know how effective their "rustication" experiment turned out to be. But most less draconian measures have shown, as a recent study by the United Nations' International Labor Organization diplomatically puts it, "rather limited success."[10]

The unabated growth of Asian cities mutely demonstrates how easily the official efforts to discourage migration can be eluded.

* * *

Who are these migrants?

Here in the leafy depths of Sumatra is an archtype of those who leave.

Sardini—like many Indonesians, he has only a single name—is a tall, slender lad with a shock of smooth, black hair and intelligent eyes.

He has all the qualifications to make him a prime candidate for migration to greener urban pastures. He is young (22 years old), a member of a poor farming family with too many mouths to feed (the eldest of four children), and equipped by training for a better life (the graduate of a technical school).

Restive young Indonesians such as him form the mainstream of the flood of rural refugees overflowing the country's cities.

The most popular destination, the capital city of Jakarta, absorbs an estimated 300 to 400 families a day. From a population of less than 500,000 in the late 1940s, Jakarta has swollen to over 7 million today.

But Sardini hasn't gone. The reason why illustrates just about the only strategy against urban migration that seems to work.

That strategy is the eminently sensible one of making the hinterlands into places where people would rather stay than leave. Backwaters of neglect like Sumatra—whose old Sanskrit name, Swarnadwipa, meant "island of gold" — must be made to glitter a little again.

That's a tall order, of course, for poor countries with precious little spare money to throw around. But it can be undertaken largely by reallocating existing funds rather than spending additional sums.

One approach is to make agricultural life attractive enough to keep folks down on the farm. Farmers can be pried out of subsistence with the aid of irrigation, higher-yielding varieties of crops, easier credit, and other services.

Another approach is to provide nonfarm work locally for the rural jobless, landless, and restless—bringing the jobs to them instead of compelling them to flee to the cities for jobs.

Such was the case with Sardini. He found a job at a new $100 million cement plant which the government lured out here to the Sumatran jungle. Its silvery metal towers rise from the green thicket of tropical vegetation like the ranked pipes of a gigantic church organ.

As one of nearly 400 production workers, Sardini earns a basic wage of 30,000 rupiahs per month (about $30). That's twice the level of subsistence which sustains nearly half of Indonesian households, mostly in rural areas.

More to the point, it far exceeds the minimum wage of 600 rupiahs per day (60 cents) which he would probably have to settle for in Jakarta.

"It's better living here," he affirms through an interpreter.

The new cement plant has all but halted the exodus to the cities from this region of south-central Sumatra. It has, in fact, reversed the population tide. The little settlement of Baturaja has become something of a jungle migration mecca.

The influx of job-seekers attracted from elsewhere on Sumatra, as well as from other, more crowded islands in the Indonesian archipelago, has tripled the town's population.

\* \* \*

His very success, however, sets Sardini apart from millions of other discontented rural Asians. A more typical urban migrant might be a Filipino named Mateo.

"Mateo from Albay," he proudly introduced himself on the day he first appeared, eager smile and freshly-cut blue uniform, as the new security guard at a small housing compound in Manila.

Not "Mateo Tanguin," or "Mateo from the security company," as a Westerner might have introduced himself.

Like millions of fellow residents of the Philippine metropolis, for Mateo the most important point of identification was his home province.

Most *manileños*, after all, have come relatively recently from one outlying province or another. A part of each of them seems never to have left. Residents of Manila ritually "go to the province" — a phrase that serves as an all-purpose explanation for any absence of a few days or more, and one that needs no further elaboration among Filipinos.

Mateo's province of Albay (pronounced, in the Spanish manner, Al-BYE) lies in the far southeastern tip of the principal island of Luzon, and ranks as one of the country's most impoverished.

His escape from a life of rural poverty came via a stint in the Philippine army, hunting anti-government guerrillas in the southern island of Mindanao.

The military training was his ticket to getting the job as a guard in Manila.

The Philippine capital bristles with security guards—not so much because of any security threat, but because they are so cheap that few property owners can afford to be without one. Hence just about any office or store, restaurant or club, apartment building or housing compound that amounts to anything—and many that don't—has its uniformed, armed guard.

Even if they don't really "guard" anything, they are rather useful to have around. They open doors, give directions, help park cars, hail taxis.

Compared with wrenching a living from the soil in Albay or lugging a pack and rifle through the jungles of Mindanao, Mateo's job at the housing compound in Manila was undemanding. He worked eight-hour shifts (seven days a week, with no meal breaks) in the little gatehouse, emerging to open and close the steel gates, and logging visitors in and out on a clipboard.

He earned 200 pesos a week (the equivalent of about $15), and shared the cramped, three-room quarters occupied by the compound caretaker, his wife, and sundry grandchildren. The pay was regular, but left nothing to be set aside as savings. And there was no job security, nor any of the benefits routinely provided in the West, such as insurance or a pension.

Mateo tackled the job with a rakish self-confidence. He fairly brandished his military bearing. When spoken to, he would draw himself up straight and cheerily bark out a response, as if addressing his company commander. He was young (24), single, and savoring what seemed to him a most cosmopolitan city.

He was soon to discover, however, the perils that await rural newcomers at the margins of Asian urban life.

Things began to come apart for Mateo after a romantic liaison with a housemaid in the compound suddenly made him a prospective father. The girl lost her job, and Mateo found himself supporting two persons on wages barely adequate for one. There were complications with the birth, and Mateo borrowed money from residents in the compound to pay the hospital bill.

But the tiny child, Mary Grace, was healthy, and no father was ever more proud. The christening—a seminal event among deeply Roman Catholic Filipino families—was scheduled for Christmas Eve.

Then, a few days before Christmas, Mateo was fired. No reason was given (or required), although grumbles had been heard that he had grown a bit careless.

He changed out of his uniform, turned in his revolver, and that was it. No explanation. No severance pay. No job.

Stunned, tears welling in his eyes, he repeated over and over to anyone who would listen:

"Christmas Eve is my baby's christening. . . ."

# ASAU, WESTERN SAMOA

By Samoan terms, Vaa Moetu leads an exotic life.

He punches the clock every day at an industrial plant.

In North America, Europe, Japan, or the rest of the industrialized world, such a workaday existence would be anything but remarkable.

But here in the South Pacific, industrial workers like Mr. Moetu are about as scarce as snowflakes.

Far off the beaten track of world commerce and too trifling a market to interest the global business magnates, this region has practically no industry.

Manufacturing generates an average of only 7 per cent of the economic output of these island nations. It provides work for just 8 per cent of the labor force.[1]

But industry is something that the South Pacific may no longer be able to afford to do without.

The case of Vaa Moetu suggests why.

The compact, 21-year-old Samoan is the eldest of seven children growing up here on the island of Savai'i, a 40-mile-wide, undulating slab of black volcanic rock cloaked in tropical rain forest.

This island is out-of-the-way even to most Samoans. Reachable only by ferry or wispy propeller-driven airplane, it is a Robinson Crusoe land of steep cliffs above crashing seas, and primeval forests broken by villages of open-sided thatched huts.

It has only one town with a commercial shopping street: two general stores, a bank, and a movie theater.

Vaa Moetu's father raises a few cattle in the kind of clan-like, village agriculture that is Samoa's economic mainstay. But booming population and declining soil and water quality are making such traditional farming less and less promising—as throughout much of Oceania.

The idle teenagers loitering in front of ice cream parlors and snack shops in the small-town capitals of many Pacific countries testify to the inability of the stagnant agricultural sector to absorb growing numbers of job-seekers.

The work force in this country of 157,000 people is expanding at a rate of over 1,500 a year.[2]

Industry is still in its infancy, but growing. A few years ago, no more than 700 Samoans were employed in manufacturing. Now 100 or so new such jobs are created every year.[3]

So Vaa Moetu, on completing school, forsook the agricultural way of life which has bound Samoans and other Pacific islanders mystically to the land for millennia.

He left the farm and landed a job at a timber mill recently built here to convert some of the island's tree cover into forest products. After a stint at the sawmill, he moved to the newly-added vaneer mill.

The tee-shirted Polynesian works at the control panel atop a hissing steel goliath that peels vaneer from logs of blond *ma'ali* wood and reddish *tava* wood, as effortlessly as unfurling a roll of paper.

He earns 75 tala (the equivalent of $50) a week—princely wealth in a country where the per capita income averages only one-seventh of that.

His non-traditional way of making a living hasn't, however, eroded his loyalty to traditional Samoan life. Through an interpreter, he says much of the money goes to help support the institutions that this society most reveres: "my family, my church, and my village."

The mill also lends no small support to his needy country.

Its exports earn Western Samoa $1.3 million a year. Only coconut exports are more lucrative.

And the mill provides jobs for 250 Samoans, making it the country's largest industrial employer.

* * *

In its industrial adolescence, Samoa isn't much different from the rest of developing Asia.

Although varying widely from one country to another, Asian industry contributes a far smaller share of economic output than in the West—about 50 per cent less.

Among Asian countries classified by the World Bank as low-income and lower middle-income, industry provides between one-fourth and one-fifth of the national gross domestic product (collectively 23 per cent in 1981).* Among industrialized market-economy countries, by contrast, industry supplies between one-third and two-fifths (36 per cent overall).

The industrial sectors of Asian countries which fall near the average, such as those of India and Pakistan, constitute only about half as large a slice of the economy as those of West Germany or Japan.[4]

As the term "nonindustrialized" implies, Asian countries as a whole remain in the cottage-industry or workshop stage of industrial development.

Small and medium-sized industries—those with 5 to 99 employees—make up over 90 per cent of all manufacturing firms and employ between one-third

---

* The figure excludes two sizeable nations—China and Indonesia—where the magnitude of industry's economic contribution (46 and 42 per cent, respectively) is untypical. Both cases spring from special circumstances: China's long campaign to develop heavy industry, and oil-rich Indonesia's petroleum industry.

and two-thirds of all manufacturing workers in the Asian countries for which data are available, according to a study by the Asian Development Bank.

Cottage industries—even smaller, often household enterprises with fewer than 5 employees—are excluded from consideration because their economic contribution is so negligible. But they are most numerous of all, comprising from 75 per cent to 95 per cent of the manufacturing establishments in these countries.[5]

In a country such as Nepal, cottage industries, in fact, are the predominant industry. Over half of industry's segment of the economic output of the Himalayan kingdom is generated by cottage industries (6 per cent out of 11 per cent). And these traditional, craft operations employ 95.6 per cent of the country's industrial workers.[6]

As in Vaa Moetu's Samoa, throughout Asia agriculture appears unable to accommodate the growing rural labor force.

It's a labor force that expanded during the 1970s, in 12 Asian countries encompassing about half of the continent's population, at the staggering rate of over 2.5 million a year.[7]

Swelling the existing labor surplus already engulfing most of the region, this helps explain why creating jobs occupies a much higher priority in the industrialization process in Asia than in the West.

In Asia, labor is often the cheapest industrial input, whereas in the West it's normally the most expensive. An Asian businessman tends to think "labor-intensive," while his Western counterpart thinks "labor-saving."

The irony is that, despite the considerable economic and social incentives, Asian industry isn't a very effective mass employer.

Except for a handful of "economic miracle" countries (Hong Kong, Singapore, South Korea, and Taiwan), industry in developing Asia contributes only about half as much to employment as it does to economic output.

For its 23 per cent average share of national economic production, industry in the low-income and lower middle-income nations provided jobs in 1980 for an average of just 12.8 per cent of the work force. Industry in the West and Japan employs, proportionately, three times as much (38 per cent).[8]

Amid a plentiful supply of cheap labor, no low-income Asian country— and precious few in any economic bracket—have managed to come up with industrial jobs for more than one out of every five persons of working age.

There is no more poignant example than India.

The world's second most populous country, and one of its poorest, has singlemindedly pursued industrialization for three decades with an investment exceeding $30 billion. The resulting capability—from steelmaking to

19

electronics to nuclear energy—ranks India as the 10th leading industrial power.

Yet industry still employs only 13 per cent of the country's bulging labor force.[9]

* * *

The problems of industrialization in Asia—and the possibilities—are found, in microcosm, here in the South Pacific.

If industry is an economic midget in Western Samoa, it's a veritable Pittsburgh by comparison with its island neighbor to the south, Tonga.

Manufacturing employs a scant 4 per cent of Tonga's work force. And, on the face of it, there's little prospect of it ever contributing much more to the national economy.

Looking for all the world like a string of floating coconut plantations, Tonga is made up largely of shelf-flat coralline islands thickly covered with coconut palms. Life revolves around a traditional Polynesian coconut-and-banana economy.

All the obstacles to industrialization found in Western Samoa loom even larger in Tonga and the other smaller island nations of the South Pacific.

Less than two-thirds as populous as Western Samoa (about 100,000) and strewn across 40,000 more square miles of ocean, Tonga offers a less promising domestic market for manufacturers. And its export markets are just as distant.

The country has no known commercially-exploitable minerals, practically no remaining forests, and not even a river or stream on its principal island.

Yet fewer places on earth have a more demonstrable need for industrialization.

Unusual among South Pacific lands, Tonga is crowded. Its population density is nearly twice as high as any of its fellow island nations. People are packed more tightly than in Pakistan or Nepal.

A unique land-tenure system entitles each adult male to an allotment of $8^{1}/_{4}$ acres of farmland. But this altruistic gesture of a 19th century Tongan king has been effectively suspended as the country has run out of land to distribute.

With virtually all arable land already being tilled, the horizons for future economic growth from agriculture are limited.

And rural landlessness is raising the number of unemployed—already high at 18 per cent of the labor force.

Hence the hopes for industrialization.

In a place like Tonga where the industrial base is so tiny, one can go a mile and a half outside the capital Nuku'alofa and take a look at a sizeable chunk of it.

Here the coconut palms have been pushed back to open up a 12-acre clearing for a cluster of 14 low, metal buildings.

This placid, sun-splashed setting is the Tongan equivalent of Germany's gritty Ruhr Valley—its industrial mainspring.

It's a mainspring that didn't exist until the government recently built this Small Industries Center.

The near-absence of suitable physical facilities for starting up a business—a sound building, well located, served by good roads and public utilities—had frustrated many a potential industrial project over the years.

The four-year-old center now houses virtually all of Tonga's export manufacturers, apart from two coconut processing plants. Its industrial tenants employ a quarter of the country's manufacturing workers.

The 14 light industries turn out a wide diversity of products—refrigerators and file cabinets, knitwear and jewelry, bicycles and wheelbarrows, toilet paper and postcards, soccer balls and wooden toys.

But all share common characteristics. They tend to use maximum labor, minimal energy, and minimal specialized technology. Their products command high market value and preferential access in neighboring Australia and New Zealand.

Inside one of the buildings, young women in Polynesian-patterned red-and-white dresses work at long rows of knitting machines producing—of all things, in this land of eternal summer—woolen sweaters.

Made of wool imported from New Zealand, the sweaters are exported to cooler climes. The firm, South Pacific Manufacturing Co. Ltd., was founded by New Zealander Louis Pogoni who, while vacationing here, noticed that Tongan girls were dexterous with their hands.

Starting four years ago with seven workers, the company now has a payroll of just over 100—making it the second largest employer in the country (after the government-owned Bank of Tonga), and the largest private employer.

In one of the center's "nursery" sheds for enterprises still in their infancy, jewelry is being fashioned from black coral gathered by divers from Tonga's encircling reefs.

Run by a brawny Tongan named Peni L. Muti, a former principal of the local high school, the firm's eight employees supply necklaces, bracelets, and earrings to Fiji's most prestigious chain of jewelry shops.

Another tenant at the center is Tonga's only manufacturer of paint, all of which previously was imported. A local joint venture with the India-based multinational Asian Paints Ltd., it employs eight islanders.

While tiny Tonga is hardly on the brink of becoming the next Taiwan or South Korea, industrialization seems to have established a toehold. Since 1975, the number of industrial enterprises has increased by nearly 50 per cent. And the number of manufacturing jobs has doubled to more than 1,000.

## SEOUL, SOUTH KOREA

Anyone looking for the roots of South Korea's "economic miracle" need look no farther, perhaps, than the bustling little factory of knob-manufacturer Jong Seon Kim.

It is entrepreneurs like Mr. Kim, as much as anyone, who have catapulted Korea from a poor, agrarian country into a world-class industrial power.

Since the early 1960s, Korea's economic output has multiplied 20-fold.[1] Per capita annual income has jumped from little more than $80 to $1,700.[2] The proportion of people living below the poverty line has fallen from about 40 per cent to about 10 per cent.[3]

Devastated by war and devoid of most natural resources, the country has built itself into a world leader in steelmaking, shipbuilding, machine tools, overseas construction, and electronics.

While giant conglomerates such as Hyundai and Daewoo are the most familiar faces in the Korean success story, thousands of anonymous small and medium-sized firms are the backbone of the country's industry.

They comprise 97 per cent of Korea's manufacturers, employ more than half of manufacturing workers, and produce over 40 per cent of the country's manufactured exports.[4]

Mr. Kim is an enterprising example.

After working in the field for a year and a half as a young college graduate, he sensed that the rising demand for household electronic products, such as television sets and stereophonic phonographs, offered great possibilities for the humble knob.

Mr. Kim struck off on his own. He founded in 1977 a company to make aluminum knobs, as well as parts for headphones and electric shavers.

He rented quarters amid the urban sprawl on the southern fringes of Seoul, installed two bench lathes, and hired five employees. He called his firm *I Hwa*, meaning "peach trees" — a picturesque if unlikely name in this grimy industrial neighborhood.

True to its name, the little business bloomed. Its knobs and other products were top quality, and found a ready market. After three years, its books bulging with more orders than it could fill, the firm was ready to expand.

But the high interest rates on commercial loans—then running at around 20 per cent—put a damper on Mr. Kim's expansion plans.

In a country like Korea, with so few natural endowments, ingenuity is often necessary for economic survival. Searching for financing he could afford, Mr. Kim heard of loans going for about half the prevailing interest rate. He applied for one.

The loan he sought was part of a $10 million pool of credit offered by the Korean government as part of a belated effort to reverse an industrialization policy long skewed in favor of a few giant combines, known as *chaebol*. The money was reserved for the most deserving small-scale industries in need of foreign currency.

Mr. Kim qualified, and got a loan of $50,000.

The loan enabled him to import six new machines, introduce two new product lines, hire six more employees, and increase production by 50 per cent. The little knob-maker was on the grow.

Riding the crest of a rising wave of Korean-made household electronic products, mounting by 20 per cent a year, the annual sales of his firm have more than quadrupled (to the equivalent of $375,000).

Now 38 years old, Mr. Kim looks less like the owner of a successful business than one of his lathe operators. His face is broad and open, his manner plain. He wears a blue polo-shirt as unpretentious as his linoleum-floored office.

As a businessman, he says, he's still learning. He accepts all the advice he can get, including managerial "extension service" from the government-owned bank that financed his expansion.

Besides his own sound business instincts and timely financial assistance, Mr. Kim's success contains several other ingredients common among his fellow entrepreneurs here.

One such element, certainly, is the celebrated Korean industriousness.

The tiny factory is a warren of activity. Under its roof are not only workshops and offices, but also dormitory lodgings for unmarried employees and rooms where the Kim family lives. Tacked on at the rear is a temporary canvas-covered working area. Space has been added as the number of employees has grown from 5 to 32.

Inside, employees regularly clock 12-hour workdays (with 4 hours of overtime) six days a week, grinding out 7,000 knobs a day and smaller quantities of push-buttons, microphone heads, electric shaver casings, and camera filter rings.

The cost of labor—commonly the largest single expense for industries in the West—amounts to little more than a quarter of Mr. Kim's costs of production.

Another factor in the success of this little company, as for the national economy as a whole, is an emphasis on exports.

Exports have fueled Korea's economic growth. The country now exports more than a quarter of its manufacturing production, with such goods making up 92 per cent of total exports.[5]

Mr. Kim's firm is even more export-oriented. Its entire output of knobs goes overseas.

Realizing from the start that his own country alone offered a limited market for electronic knobs, Mr. Kim set his entrepreneurial sights outward. He arranged to supply knobs to large Korean electronics companies—now 10 of them—to be fitted on products which are shipped throughout the world.

Despite the headlong plunge into the electronic age on a global scale, touches of the old Korea endure.

Upon entering the factory, everyone exchanges his shoes for straw sandals. And Mr. Kim's secretary does her computations not on a calculator—which Korea exports by the millions—but on a wooden abacus.

Not all Korean small and medium-sized manufacturers have done as well as Mr. Kim. Others have done better.

But the economic energy collectively generated by the more than 30,000 of these "Mr. Kims" may provide an insight into how this country has been able to pull off its "miracle."

# Getting Enough Food to Eat

ASHUGANJ, BANGLADESH

For one of the world's poorest countries, the Bangladesh countryside looks deceptively plenteous.

The table-flat landscape is thickly carpeted with rice — some green, other golden brown and being cut, handful by handful, by women in brightly-colored saris.

Amid groves of luxuriant banana plants, villages of bamboo huts cling to man-made hillocks that protect them from the constant threat of floods in a country that is basically the delta of two of the world's great rivers, the Ganges and the Brahmaputra.

But any impression of abundance quickly fades at the sight of the first tin begging bowl.

Battered shapeless and worn dull, the bowls are thrust through the open windows of passenger trains at every stop on a journey through the same farmland that exudes such bounty.

At the end of the outstretched arm clutching each begging bowl lies an imploring face etched with the wan, hollow-eyed look of hunger.

The passengers packed inside the train — as well as on the roofs and over the couplings between the old red coaches — look only marginally better off.

The fact is that Bangladesh does not come even close to feeding itself.

Its plodding progress on increasing foodgrain production, averaging 1.5 per cent a year over the past decade, is (quite literally) swallowed up by population growth over the same span at the rate of 2.4 per cent a year.[1]

With 99 million people already jammed into a country about the size of the American state of Wisconsin, Bangladesh in the past six years alone has

generated 14 million additional mouths to feed—more than the entire population of Australia.[2]

Ask a Bangladeshi villager what he eats, and he describes two meals a day
of rice. In the morning there is puffed rice and a molasses-like syrup called
*gur*, and in the evening boiled rice and fish. Chicken is an occasional treat.
Beef is even rarer—once a year during the autumn observance of Moslem
Charity Day (*Eid-ul-Azha*) when cattle are sacrificed.[3]

In stark statistical terms, the average Bangladeshi eats during the course of
a year about as much meat as one good-sized Sunday roast on an American
family dining table—7 pounds. His yearly diet also includes less than 3
gallons of milk and just 17 eggs.[4]

Bangladeshis wear the results of generations of such malnutrition. The
government has calculated that the country's average 18-year-old male stands
about 5 feet, 3 inches tall and weighs 97 pounds.[5]

\* \* \*

Getting enough food to eat is something that few Westerners worry much
about.

Quite the opposite. Overeating and overweightness loom as far more
consuming concerns. One of every five adults in industrialized countries are
reckoned by the World Health Organization to be overweight.[6] Obesity has
ballooned into a major health problem in the West, and millions of dollars are
spent to undo the effects of overindulgence at the dining table.

Most people in developing Asia, on the other hand, live on an enforced
low-calorie diet. Those "millions of starving children in Asia" — held up to
generations of Western youngsters to shame them into finishing their
meals—are all too real.

There are, in fact, 300 million people in Asia slowly "starving" of chronic
undernourishment, according to the United Nations' World Food Council.[7]
Another 300 million are merely malnourished.[8]

With human pressure so heavy on available food resources, it's a wonder
that Asia feeds as many mouths as it does.

The continent supporting over half of the world's population contains only
one-third of the world's arable land. Its "land-to-man" ratio of just under half
an acre is the lowest on the globe.[9]

The typical Asian farm occupies little more than the barnyard of a Western
farm. The average farm size in France is 64 acres, in Britain 163 acres, and in
the more-spacious United States 431 acres.[10] In Asia, 40 per cent of all farms
cover less than two and a half acres (one hectare) and 90 per cent are less than
12 acres (five hectares).[11]

One compensation for such closely-attended farmlets would be expected to be high productivity. Alas, not. Even the highest-yielding agriculture in monsoon Asia—Japan—is only one-quarter as productive per worker as American farming.[12]

Most of these tiny plots, moreover, are hopelessly vulnerable to the vagaries of the Asian elements.

They rely on rainfall—as does 60 per cent of the acreage growing the staple crop of rice[13]—when irrigation would bring year-round cultivation and an additional crop to reap every year during the dry season.

They receive little fertilizer, when more would almost guarantee higher yields. Farmers in low-income Asian countries apply about one-quarter as much fertilizer per acre of tillable land as do their colleagues in industrialized countries in the West and Japan, according to the World Bank.[14]

Unable to raise enough of its own food, Asia relies hungrily on imports. Despite a string of good harvests and great strides toward self-sufficiency, the continent's major importers were collectively shipping in just about as much grain in the mid-1980s as they had a decade earlier.[15]

* * *

Every night, from the flickering, bluish glow of television sets across Bangladesh, wafts the catchy jingle of a commercial for "Ovacon," a birth-control pill.

Advertisements for the same contraceptive—with its promise of "a carefree and exuberant married life" — are prominent on the country's radio stations and in its newspapers.

More-dour warnings about overpopulation are heard from government officials almost as frequently.

Too few are convinced. Every day 10,000 babies are born in Bangladesh.[16]

In the world's most densely-inhabited country, such population growth imposes a double strain on agricultural resources. Not only does it produce additional people to feed, but additional heirs among whom to further subdivide farms already small.

Islamic law dictates that family land be divided and passed along to each child. The result is something the Koran never anticipated: slivers of land which are too tiny to support a family, or which are sold to larger landowners—thereby swelling the numbers of landless.

Losing one's land is often the first downward step into the ranks of what is known in Bangladesh as the *bittaheen*, or resourceless people—that underclass of the very poorest who possess virtually nothing to call their own.

In this overwhelmingly rural country, where 89 per cent of the population lives in the countryside, nearly one out of every three households (29 per cent) owns no land. Half (48 per cent) own two acres or less. Thus more than three-quarters of Bangladeshis (77 per cent) either own no land or only a patch of marginal size.[17]

The size of the average farm here has shrunk from 3.5 acres in 1977 to 2.4 acres now, and is still contracting.[18]

The rice grown on these farms is among the lowest-yielding in Asia.

One reason is the paucity of irrigation. Although two-thirds of tillable land is suitable for irrigation, barely 20 per cent now has such facilities.[19]

The rest is ravaged by alternating cycles of floods and droughts severe even by Asian standards. Every year an average of 12 million acres of farmland — one-third of the entire country — are flooded beneath 12 to 15 feet of water. Another 3 million acres along the coasts are inundated by seawater. But when the dry season comes, the rivers shrivel up to mere trickles, losing 95 per cent of their water.[20]

As if this weren't punishment enough, Bangladesh cropland is meagerly fertilized. Fertilizer is applied, per acre, at only about half the average worldwide level.[21] It is, for one thing, too expensive. Most must be imported.

Small, close-to-the-line farmers cannot afford fertilizer. And neither can the large number of sharecroppers, who split their harvests half-and-half with the landowner but bear the costs of production themselves.

It's a pity. Urea fertilizer, combined with faster-maturing varieties of rice seeds (which also cost a bit more), can elicit three crops per year instead of the usual two.

That's why farmers who can find the money are willing to pay black-market prices for scarce urea.

Bangladesh's rice may be better fertilized in coming years.

Two fertilizer factories now being built, with generous doses of international assistance, should enable the country by the late 1980s to meet all its own fertilizer needs.

The one here at Ashuganj in central Bangladesh will take advantage of the country's practically only exploitable mineral resource — a nearby field of natural gas — to produce 2,600 tons per day of urea and ammonia fertilizers.

Another fertilizer plant is rising at Chittagong in eastern Bangladesh.

Cheaper, domestic fertilizer will help, but the food gap in Bangladesh is expected to remain wide.

To fill it — and the empty stomachs — the country has imported in the past five years an average of 1.6 million tons of foodgrains a year.[22] That's roughly

34 pounds for every man, woman, and each of those 10,000 daily newborn babies.

Bangladesh's begging bowls seem unlikely to soon disappear.

## TALUNGAGUNG, INDONESIA

A diminutive Indonesian with a wispy mustache, and the single name of Suprapto, is part of one of the giant successes of the century.

No lofty statesman, or bemedaled general, or billionaire industrialist, Suprapto is a simple farmer.

But his accomplishment, and that of millions like him, affects the lives of far more Asians than the more-celebrated exploits of the rich and mighty.

He and his faceless fellow farmers in other parts of the continent are lifting some countries, once among the least capable of feeding themselves, toward self-sufficiency in food.

How? Through a variety of means, including their own ingenuity and hard work.

Suprapto owes much of his new-found success to the mound of earth beneath his feet: the high bank of an irrigation trench. It courses, from where he stands, across a green, flat valley floor that stretches like a lush carpet from one volcanic-ridged horizon to the other.

This is the Brantas River basin in East Java—an important granary of the world's fifth most populous country, and long its largest rice importer. Yet this verdant valley is overburdened by population and, until recently, abused by a fickle climate.

Suprapto is one of some 57,000 farmers in this part of the valley. Their average cropland is less than two-thirds of an acre, or smaller than many American housing lots.

For generations, they reaped but two low-yielding crops each year—rice in the wet season, and in the dry season *palawija*, a term encompassing corn, soybeans, peanuts, cassava, and assorted vegetables. The resulting earnings often fell short of meeting basic family needs.

Dressed up in his Sunday-best checked sportshirt and narrow-brimmed fedora, the middle-aged Suprapto proudly tells a visitor of the changes brought by the arrival of irrigation in the late 1970s.

Farmers in these parts speak of the coming of irrigation in the same historical terms that American farmers attach to the invention of the cotton gin or the grain combine. And with justification.

No longer dependent on rainfall, Suprapto now raises three crops per

29

year—two crops of rice and one of *palawija*—instead of two. Yields of paddy (unhulled rice) have jumped from about 1 ton per acre to about 3 tons, and yields of *palawija* have doubled from 800 pounds per acre to 1,600 pounds. His income has risen accordingly.

"Before," he says, motioning toward the dense stalks of rice being weeded behind him, "the land was dry and there would be no trace of crops at this time of year."

* * *

Not long ago, Indonesia was one of the world's agricultural "basket cases."

For much of its 39 years of nationhood, the former Dutch East Indies has been the globe's most voracious importer of rice. The 500,000 tons which it imported annually in the 1950s had grown to an average of 1.7 million tons a year by the second half of the 1970s. In 1977, imports reached 2 million tons—rice enough to feed 9 million people.[1]

Indonesia was importing one-tenth of its basic food requirements. The cost exceeded $1 billion a year, roughly half of it for rice.[2]

Masked by these grim statistics, meanwhile, changes were afoot out in the country's crowded rice paddies. Herculean efforts were being made among the 30 million farmers like Suprapto, who comprise over half of the national work force, to remedy this agricultural failing.

Newly-developed "miracle" strains of rice—offering higher yields and greater resistance to pests and diseases—were spreading from valley to valley. Spurred by a government price ceiling, fertilizer consumption per acre during the 1970s quintupled.[3] Some $1.5 billion was invested in irrigation systems, giving Indonesia the highest proportion of arable land under irrigation in Southeast Asia (about two-fifths).[4]

Results were a little slow in coming. The World Bank, for one, pessimistically predicted that Indonesia would still rely on rice imports until 1990.[5]

But rice production was gradually increasing, and by the dawning of the 1980s it had effectively doubled. Whereas in the early 1970s the country harvested 12 million tons of rice a year, in the present decade crops have exceeded 20 million tons by a steadily widening margin, reaching 26 million tons in 1985.[6]

Only a quarter of the increase in rice output has come from an expansion in cultivated land. The remaining three-quarters has come from rising productivity.[7] Some 80 per cent of rice now harvested is the high-yielding variety.[8]

Indonesia stopped importing rice in 1981,[9] and imported only relatively small amounts the next year, chiefly to build up its stockpiles.[10]

The worst drought in a decade forced imports to be resumed in 1983 on a scale reminiscent of the 1970s (1.2 million tons), but it appears to have been only a temporary setback.[11] The token tonnage imported since then was largely ordered before the record-breaking size of the latest harvests was known, or else to supply special varieties not grown domestically.

For nearly a decade, production of rice had been growing twice as fast as consumption (5.1 per cent *vs.* 2.6 per cent a year). By 1984 production drew even and then sped ahead, in a milestone as significant as any in the country's history.[12]

The world's largest rice importer as recently as a few years ago, Indonesia is now self-sufficient in its staple food. Not only that, but it has turned exporter — selling small shipments to the Philippines and African nations.[13]

The one-time "basket case" has become something of a case study in agricultural success.

\* \* \*

Fortunately for a lot of hungry Asians, Indonesia isn't alone in its new food-producing proficiency.

In Asia as a whole, the Food and Agriculture Organization of the United Nations reported in 1983 that — for the first time since records have been kept — food production was outpacing population growth.[14]

During the 1970s, the average annual rate of increase in food output exceeded that of population in countries as diverse as Burma, China, India, Indonesia, Malaysia, Pakistan, Philippines, Sri Lanka, and Thailand.[15]

No food is more important to Asians than rice. About 90 per cent of the world's rice is grown and consumed on this continent. It makes up between 60 per cent and 80 per cent of Asians' calorie intake.[16] The average Filipino, for instance, eats 213 pounds of rice a year.[17]

So synonymous is rice with eating that, in Japanese, the word for meal (*gohan*) is the same as the word for rice.

Production of this Asian staff of life has increased, continent-wide, by about 50 per cent over the past 15 years.[18] Rice output grew more during these few years than in the preceding 7,000.[19]

Such are the waymarks of the march of the so-called "Green Revolution" across Asia.

A series of hybrid varieties of rice — IR-8, IR-36, IR-42, IR-56, and the newest IR-58, bearing the prefix of the International Rice Research Institute in the Philippines where they were bred — now occupy at least a quarter of the continent's rice fields.[20]

They can generate two or three times as much rice per acre as traditional strains, under proper care and conditions. They ward off insects and viruses. They have steadily reduced the maturity period, from 135 days for early hybrids down to 95 to 100 days, enabling a farmer to squeeze three crops into a year instead of the customary two.[21]

Yet Asia's farmers, who have been growing rice for thousands of years, needed strong persuasion at first to switch.

Since the new rice had shorter stems than the old high-head varieties, farmers had to stoop to cut it. The shorter stems also meant less rice straw to feed cattle and buffalo. Farmers complained, too, that the new rice wasn't as tasty. But the bumper yields eventually convinced them.

Besides "miracle" rice, the most crucial requirement for multiple cropping is an adequate and timely supply of water—meaning, in most cases, irrigation. Although only about a third of Asia's arable land is irrigated, it produces half of the continent's food.[22]

In some parts of the world, irrigation has acquired a rather checkered reputation. Bigger yields sometimes have been accompanied, notably in Africa, by damaging side-effects such as waterlogged fields and the surfacing of salt from the soil.

But the special character of Asian agriculture seems tailor-made for irrigation. The problems that have plagued irrigation elsewhere have largely spared Asia.

One reason appears to be the relative abundance of water in most parts of the continent, except arid regions of India and Pakistan. This tends to minimize the salinization problem. Another reason may be an ironic blessing bestowed by overpopulation and land scarcity. The tiny size of Asian farms, together with the labor-intensive cultivation, encourage careful water management.[23]

With invaluable farm aids such as these, a number of Asian nations now find themselves strikingly better able to feed themselves. Among them:

## INDIA

The shining example is probably this country so long associated with famine and starvation.

Twenty years ago India was the world's second largest food importer, averting hunger of disastrous proportions by importing 10 million tons of various types of grain a year. As recently as 1978, it was still importing 4 million to 6 million tons.[24]

Today India is, for all practical purposes, agriculturally self-sufficient—an achievement that may rank as the country's greatest material accomplishment since independence.

In the past 30 years, it has increased production of rice, its principal cereal, two and a half times over.[25] The output of wheat—the most stunning success of the country's Green Revolution—has risen so steeply that more than a fifth of the last crop was squirreled away in warehouses.[26]

India's buffer stocks are overflowing, and it has ventured into the international grain market—as a seller, for a change, instead of a buyer.[27]

## CHINA

The country with the world's largest number of eaters has brought off a provisioning feat of similarly prodigious proportions.

With population growing and arable land shrinking—20 million fewer acres, or only half as much cropland per person as in the early 1950s—China seemed doomed to permanent reliance on food handouts and grain imports.[28]

Since the late 1970s, however, high-yielding and other hybrid varieties have spread to half of the country's ricelands and have come to dominate wheat and corn farming.[29]

Overall agricultural output has risen at a rate of nearly 8 per cent a year. Grain production, pausing only for a drought in the early 1980s, has mounted almost 50 per cent.[30]

The country has become essentially self-supporting in grain, and even exports small quantities of corn to Japan and elsewhere. It now faces a problem of plenty: how to transport and store its unaccustomed surpluses.[31]

## PAKISTAN

India's and China's western neighbor is almost as bright an agricultural success story.

Pakistan once appeared hopelessly dependent on food imports. In the late 1970s it still imported some 2 million tons of wheat a year. Yet Pakistan is now approaching self-sufficiency in food. It has become a wheat exporter and the world's third largest rice exporter.[32]

## PHILIPPINES

This Southeast Asian food-deficit nation also is flirting with self-reliance.

After the alarming spectre of shortages in the early 1970s, rice production began to grow at an annual rate (over 5 per cent) nearly two-thirds higher than in the 1960s.[33] The improvement enabled the country to switch from a major importer of rice to a marginal exporter in 1977.

After four years of shipments to Latin America, Western Europe, and other parts of Asia, exports were halted, but the Philippines remains very near self-sufficiency.[34]

## BURMA

The case of Burma is a little different. Traditionally blessed with ample food for its needs, the country's rice production had deteriorated to the point where scarcity touched off serious social unrest in 1974.[35]

Since then, some $300 million has been invested in introducing high-yielding varieties of rice. They now cover over half of Burma's rice acreage, and are producing rich dividends.[36]

Rice output is spurting. The country is growing more than twice as much rice as in pre-war colonial days. The main shortage now is storage space for its bumper harvests — heaped at times even in schoolrooms, pagodas, and monasteries.

Burma has become a major world rice supplier, and the commodity comprises nearly half of its total exports.[37]

National "self-sufficiency" in food doesn't necessarily mean, of course, that a country's people are sufficiently fed. The mere production, on a per capita basis, of enough food for all doesn't assure that the food is available to people or that they can afford to buy it.

Millions have remained malnourished in nations such as India and the Philippines while they exported grain.[38]

But food self-sufficiency offers a poor, developing country at least the opportunity — and perhaps its only opportunity — to meet this most basic of human needs.

## SAMUT SAKORN, THAILAND

Thailand is often called an aquatic country — and nowhere more aptly so than here.

This sea-hugging province south of Bangkok sometimes seems unsure whether it's part of the Asian mainland or the Gulf of Thailand.

The land lies level as a lake-bed, just inches above the sea, a treeless expanse of grassy swamps and grey mud-flats.

Life circulates around rivers and canals. They are the traffic arteries. People skim along them in slender, pointy-prowed wooden longboats. Cargo glides in convoys of tin-roofed barges.

Along the banks, residents ply their trades, do their marketing, gossip with their neighbors, and raise their families in thatched grass houses.

For years, this transitional zone where Thailand recedes gently into the sea has supported little more than a modest production of salt by evaporating sea-water in shallow ponds.

But its split personality of half-land, half-sea ideally suits another livelihood far more promising: fish farming.

Just how promising is shown by a slight farmer in a disheveled blue shirt and black sarong named Tone Biromjeng. Despite a look of wariness in his slit eyes and dour mouth, twisted open at one corner, his willingness to try something new belies his 76 years.

Extracting a marginal income from this land for most of his life by raising vegetables, he switched 10 years ago to raising shrimp in ponds. His return was little better until an international team of experts and money recently turned up to acquaint him with intensified shrimp-farming.

Using a waterpump, shrimp seeds, and feed in his two ponds of just under an acre each, Mr. Biromjeng has been able to harvest two crops of shrimp per year, instead of just one.

The income for his household of seven has jumped by nearly 50 per cent (from 80,000 baht or about $3,500, to over 118,000 baht or $5,000 a year). And his pump-priming loan of 60,000 baht (about $2,600) was paid off in just one year.

* * *

Fish farming, of course, is much more than a way of enriching subsistence farmers like Tone Biromjeng.

Fish and fish products constitute the cheapest source of animal protein for much of humanity, including millions who simply cannot afford meat. Thais, for example, draw more than 60 per cent of their animal protein from fish. And some people less aquatic than the Thais, such as Malaysians and Filipinos, eat even more fish per person.[1]

But this staple food is in diminishing supply. Under assault by heavier fishing, more efficient fishing methods, and pollution, catches of fish from the world's oceans peaked in 1970.[2]

In the case of Thailand, the resources of ocean-bottom fish in the waters off its shores—the Gulf of Thailand and the Andaman Sea—are now believed to be fully exploited.[3]

Any future increase in fish for the world's growing population seems destined to come from the land—harvested, much like any soil crop, through aquaculture.

Aquaculture is far from new. It has been an important source of food in China, for instance, for centuries. But its potential seems barely scratched. Barely one-tenth of all fish consumed is now farmed.[4]

Here in Asia, the continent with the most mouths to feed, aquaculture is—perhaps out of necessity—furthest developed. Nearly 85 per cent of the world fish-farming production (8 million of 9.5 million tons) is reared in Asia.

All signs point to a steady increase. External loans for aquaculture projects in the region are reported by the United Nations' Food and Agriculture Organization to have more than tripled in three years (to $53 million).[5]

The output of fish from aquaculture in Asia's developing countries was expected to double in the 10-year span between 1975 and 1985, and then perhaps quintuple by the end of the century.

Fish farming is being developed in a systematic way in virtually every country in Asia—from the industrialized city-states of Hong Kong and Singapore, to poor rural lands such as Bangladesh and Nepal.[6]

For some of them, it all seems to be happening none too soon.

In Bangladesh, where UNICEF recently implanted the first aquaculture to be successful on a large scale, population has grown by 22 per cent over the past eight years while fish production has grown by only 1 per cent. Fish has disappeared from the tables of all but the most prosperous homes, and malnutrition has worsened.[7]

In Sri Lanka, where the government is trying to triple inland fish production, the per capita consumption of fish—the sole source of protein for 60 per cent of the people—has dropped by one-quarter since 1970 due to shortages.[8] The island nation imports $5 million worth of fish a year despite being surrounded by sea.[9]

\* \* \*

The growth of aquaculture in Asia takes forms as simple as a small fish pond behind a farmhouse, and as sophisticated as the 13,000-tons-a-year prawn farm—the world's largest—now being built in the Malaysian state of Sabah on the island of Borneo.[10]

Besides shrimps and prawns, the common output are that ancient mainstay of Chinese aquaculture, the carp, plus mackerel-like milkfish, and spiny-finned *tilapia*, originally from Africa.[11]

One of the more imaginative concepts combines the raising of fish, livestock, and grain in an integrated farming operation. The various components support each other in an all-but-self-sufficient little enterprise that makes nearly complete use of its own resources while eliminating waste.

Agricultural by-products unusable by humans are fed to farm animals and fish; animal manure fertilizes fish ponds; water drained from fish ponds irrigates cropland.

The Chinese, who are old hands at fish farming, mix into their integrated operations a bewildering variety of ingredients.

Fish are fed waste from sources as diverse as sugar cane, silkworms, mulberry leaves, mushroom subsoil, soybeans, peanuts, and farmyard livestock such as pigs, cattle, sheep, horses, ducks, and geese.

Soil from the bottom of the fishpond, in turn, is used to fertilize crops ranging from sugar cane to mulberry trees whose leaves feed silkworms.

Using a self-contained system such as this, the average fish farmer in China's Pearl River delta harvests 2 tons of fish per acre of water—triple the yield of American aquaculture operations run along traditional lines.[12]

One place where the integrated system is being introduced is Thailand's central plains—sprawling tableland and empty skies where it seems as if the whole world is nothing but endless rice fields.

Buonchong Disayanan, a sturdy 48-year-old with a knot of thick black hair, has tended his family's 16 acres of rice here ever since he became old enough to join his father in the fields. His labors have earned him no better than a modest living, grossing 60,000 baht (about $2,600) a year.

When he heard about integrated farming, and its early success among a couple of local farmers, he was understandably interested.

With the aid of loan money and know-how supplied by the Thai government and foreign aid, he recently converted several acres of his rice fields into two ponds for fish and prawns. A roofed enclosure between the ponds awaits the arrival of 30 pigs.

Others among the 23 participating members of his farmers' cooperative are raising ducks (instead of pigs) with their fish, prawns, and rice.

Many more local farmers would like to switch from rice-growing to integrated aquaculture, but cannot. Their farms are too remote from the roads and canals needed to market the harvests from the more intensified operations.

Mr. Disayanan's place itself is hardly at the crossroads of commerce. It is reached on deeply-rutted gravel roads, and then by a bamboo raft poled across a canal awash with children and water buffalo seeking refuge from the heat.

Although still waiting for his first harvest from integrated farming, Mr. Disayanan has reason to be optimistic. A neighbor who pioneered the raising of pigs and prawns boosted his annual income by 30,000 baht (about $1,300).

Thousands of Thai farmers like Buonchong Disayanan and Tone Biromjeng are beginning to farm fish. And the additional fish that they are anticipated to produce will meet the annual fish demand of hundreds of thousands of Thais.

In a not-so-small way, aquaculture is helping renew the traditional concept of prosperity expressed by an old Thai saying: "There is rice in the field and fish in the river."

# Where Essentials of Life Are Luxuries

## KALUDHER, PAKISTAN

Like many villages in this mountain-ribbed northern tip of Pakistan, Kaludher lacks so much as a road—or even a trail wide enough for a cart—linking it with the outside world.

It is reached only by a 15-minute walk from the nearest dirt road on muddy footpaths along irrigation trenches. The paths border small fields where towering stalks of sugar cane are being harvested by hand. Other fields are velvety green with winter wheat.

The village itself is a scattering of farmhouse complexes surrounded by mud walls. The walls enclose living quarters with thatched roofs, and open courtyards often containing a well and baked-mud fireplace for cooking.

As remote as Kaludher is, however, a wire strung atop a row of stubby metal utility poles attests to one important modern amenity: electricity. The village was plugged a few months ago into the electrical age.

Not that the place is suddenly athrob with television sets, tape decks, and microwave ovens. A few bare lightbulbs is all that anyone can afford. Life is still spartan and harsh.

But even so rudimentary a refinement as electricity was available until recently only in cities, despite the fact that Asia remains predominantly a society of rural villages.

Now some of these "city" comforts are beginning to reach the villages where three-quarters of Asians live.

The long deprivation is slowly giving way as new attention—and money—are directed to rural uplift. The impetus is perhaps not so much altruistic as pragmatic: stimulating greater food production, and improving living conditions to keep villagers from migrating to cities already hopelessly overcrowded.

The changes are visible in villages—even some of the least accessible—across the vast sweep of the world's most populous continent.

In few of them, however, has it taken as much doing as in the village of Kaludher.

First, the world's largest earth-filled hydroelectric dam was built across the Indus River 15 miles to the south.

When the time came to connect Kaludher to the national grid, the wire, poles, and other transmission gear had to be lugged to the village on foot.

One villager to benefit from the undertaking is Ghulam Sarwar, a farmer whose weathered face is accented by a greying mustache and framed by a white skullcap and woolen shawl.

Sitting on heavy wooden cots with rope seats in traditional village fashion, Mr. Sarwar tells a group of visitors that the house and its 15 occupants—his family and his brother's—now have electric lights for the first time.

He motions toward a barren field adjoining the house. This tract, now untillable, will be brought into cultivation by the electric water-pump which he says he plans to install to irrigate it.

The new cropland will boost the output of sugar cane, wheat, and tobacco which he grows on his 25 acres.

The 21-year-old son of his nearest neighbor welcomes the coming of electricity for a different reason.

Wrapped in a beige shawl like his fellow villagers, Rahamdali—he has only this single name—radiates the earnestness that characterizes college students the world over.

Enrolled at a nearby rural institute, he found kerosene lamps provided inadequate light for his homework. Their fumes, he adds, were not only obnoxious but unhealthy, particularly in wintertime when the house was closed up for warmth.

Ten lightbulbs now dangle from the house's mud walls and ceiling timbers. And, with a monthly household light bill of 15 rupees (about $1.30), electricity works out to be cheaper than kerosene.

* * *

Electricity may be taken for granted in the Western industrialized countries as a basic necessity of life available to virtually everyone.

But few rural homes in Asia have ever been illuminated at night by anything more than a candle or oil lamp. India and Thailand have electrified barely a third of their villages. In Bangladesh, Sri Lanka, and Indonesia, the figure ranges only between 3 per cent and 7 per cent.[1]

The simple kerosene "bottle lamp" used in millions of Asian homes emits woefully insufficient illumination for reading. For proper light, any reading must be done within two feet of the lamp.

What it does emit, all too profusely, are dangerous quantities of carbon monoxide, soot, and fumes of unburnt kerosene. Furthermore, the lamp poses a considerable fire hazard.

Keeping it fueled (according to a recent study in Sri Lanka) often costs rural families 30 per cent of their household income — several times more than city families pay for electric lighting.[2]

In a country like Pakistan, where electricity is still unknown in much of the rural region where three out of four Pakistanis live, the arrival of this seemingly magical form of energy is an event that transforms lives.

It brightens the gloom of centuries of lamp-lit nights in rural Pakistan homes. In this dimness illiteracy flourishes, still reaching well over 75 per cent in the countryside, and few villagers, like Rahamdali, clamber their way into college.[3]

Electricity can help a farmer improve chronically low crop yields through an electrically-powered irrigation pump that assures his fields an adequate supply of water.

Indigenously-generated electricity also helps this poor country (average annual per capita income: about $350) cope with a growing demand for power without swelling its oil import bill, already a heavy drain on the economy.

Lights are twinkling on in a steadily advancing number of villages across Asia. More than $1 billion have been spent on rural electrification by the continent's developing countries, an outlay that is growing at the rate of 20 per cent a year.[4]

It's no panacea. Rural electrification has had a tough time fulfilling all the claims made for it by overzealous engineers and planners.

It hasn't always financially benefited the rural poor very much, nor been harnessed effectively for agricultural production, concludes a study by the United Nations' International Labor Organization.

Yet it can be an important economic catalyst. In India, the spread of electric power into the countryside tripled agriculture's share of the nation's electricity consumption between 1960 and 1980 (from 5 per cent to 15 per cent). The number of electrical irrigation pumps increased six-fold, from less than 500,000 to 3.6 million.

There is little hard evidence that rural electrification retards rural migration to the cities. It doubtlessly improves the quality of village life, but electrifying farm chores inevitably displaces some rural labor.

Birth rates seem to drop when electricity is introduced, as suggested by studies in Pakistan and Thailand. But a cause-and-effect relationship is difficult to establish.[5]

Whether or not it lives up to its promise fully everywhere, few dispute that the advent of electricity is anything but a blessing to the village lit up—an amenity almost universally welcomed by the villagers.

The electrification of Kaludher was repeated in 7,000 Pakistan villages during the past five years—more than the total electrified in the previous 30 years.[6] The scale of the program was made possible, government officials feel, by the added power supplied by the huge Tarbela hydroelectric dam project near here.

Even amid the many natural wonders of this corner of the Indian subcontinent where the great Indus River emerges from the western shoulder of the Himalayas, the Tarbela dam is an impressive sight.

An expanse of grey stone as tall as a 40-story building (470 feet) and a mile and a half long, it collects the waters of the Indus in a shimmery blue reservoir that stretches 60 miles back into the mountains.

The physical size of the project is matched by its statistical dimensions.

Still just partially finished, Tarbela supplies over half of Pakistan's electricity. It is already capable of generating 1,600 megawatts—more than the entire generating capacity of many other Asian countries. By completion in 1991, a total of 17 generators will nearly triple the present maximum output.

Work has been underway at Tarbela for 15 years, and the ultimate cost is expected to exceed $1.5 billion. That's a lot of money, but Pakistan pays that much for imported oil every year.

The reception accorded the project in this power-hungry country is expressed by the words from the Koran, inscribed in giant Urdu script and English lettering in white rocks on the face of the dam: "And He hath made the rivers of service unto you."

\* \* \*

Far from the windswept heights of the Indian subcontinent, thousands of miles away in the steamy lowlands of Southeast Asia, is another example of a village getting a first taste of urban amenities.

The village of Dong Pong in Thailand is as different as it is distant from Kaludher in Pakistan.

Clustered rather than scattered, its houses are built of wood instead of mud, and designed to draw ventilation, not ward it off—raised one story above the ground and filled with unglassed windows.

The dirt lane that winds among the houses leads to an arched gateway, resplendent in carved reliefs painted white, orange, and green, gleaming ethereally amid the weathered drabness of the village. It is the entrance to the village Buddhist temple.

The village and its temple are an island of acacia-shaded habitation in a sea of rice fields, their waist-high stalks dipping gently in the moist tropical breeze.

This is northeastern Thailand—the least developed region in a country where the average annual per capita income is only $770.

The exigencies of life here rest amiably, however, on Thai Puidang. A squarish-built villager with a greying brush-cut, he has eyes that twinkle and a ready smile that unveils teeth stained red by decades of chewing betel nuts.

After a hot day in the rice fields, he is squatting, clad in a plaid sarong and blue rubber sandals, on a wooden platform-bench in the open area underneath his elevated house. His wife is weaving at a loom nearby.

The scene is a timeless one. For centuries, Thai villagers have relaxed like this beneath their upraised houses as the day's shadows lengthened. But a closer look reveals subtle touches of modernity.

The house overhead, for a start. It's new, and roomier than the traditional Thai country home. With obvious pride, Mr. Puidang explains that he recently built it to replace a house only one-third as large.

Inside, it boasts luxuries once undreamed of. There's an electric fan to make the heat of the tropics a little less stifling. And there's a television set to make the long village evenings a little less empty.

The creature comforts are the trappings of a new-found prosperity. The introduction of irrigation has nearly doubled the income from Mr. Puidang's 7.5-acre farm, to 20,000 baht or about $870 a year.

Other newly-irrigated farmers in Dong Pong also are savoring their rise out of subsistence. The village is sprinkled with refrigerators, radios, television sets, and motor scooters.

And, in a region where a farmer's most prized possession is usually a water buffalo, Mr. Puidang's son, a duck farmer, owns a shiny new pickup truck.

## BANGKOK, THAILAND

Pimol Chame is immersing himself these days in a new-found luxury: a bath.

If he were a remote villager or a shantytown squatter, the novelty of having running water for bathing would be unremarkable.

But Mr. Chame is a professional man—a retired schoolteacher—living in one of Asia'a major capitals.

He and his family occupy a small but comfortable house in the district of Thonburi, which means literally "money town," although most of the government and wealth gravitated long ago to the more fashionable side of the Chao Phraya River.

The little house lies up a quiet back street called Soi Mitrpatana, just around the corner from a neighborhood incense-maker—a batch of slender incense sticks spread neatly to dry in the courtyard sun.

Although the home has municipal water service, for years it was served up precious little water. In daytime the pipes were empty. The family used to crawl out of bed in the middle of the night to draw water when the pressure was higher. But even then, the faucets usually yielded barely a trickle.

"Bathing," says the sober retiree, maintaining his teacherly dignity clad only in a pair of brown shorts, "was out of the question."

His neighbors recount similar hardships. Indeed, until recently, low water pressure was common throughout much of Bangkok, depriving wide areas of water for hours or even days. Families who could afford to do so installed private pumps and storage tanks. Others bought bottled water from vendors.

Having ballooned in population from 1 million to 6 million since as recently as the mid-1950s—fed by a tide of rural migrants now estimated to number as many as 1,000 a day—the Thai capital simply outgrew its water system.[1]

And low pressure may not be the worst of it.

The 300 million gallons of groundwater pumped daily from beneath the city by 10,000 public and private wells is blamed (along with the urban buildup above) for the alarming sinkage of Bangkok at the rate of nearly 4 inches per year into the low floodplain on which it is built. Monsoon rains already leave some sections under water for up to three months of the year.[2]

* * *

A supply of safe water, piped into the home, is just as elusive a commodity in most other metropolises on this teeming continent.

In Manila, the sight of people lugging plastic buckets and jugs from street-side spigots and fire hydrants testifies to the fact that one-third of the residents of the Philippine capital—some 2 million people—lack their own source of water.[3]

In Karachi, little more than one house in three has a water connection. Even so, Pakistan's largest city (estimated population: 6 million) is pumped barely half as much water as city officials say it needs—a need that is growing by 10 million gallons a year.[4]

In Jakarta, only 10 per cent of the Indonesian capital's nearly 7 million inhabitants can rely on city water service. Thousands of artesian wells are depleting its underground reservoirs, and drinking water is now trucked daily from the mountains.[5]

And yet the cities are just about the only places in Asia—a region still overwhelmingly rural—where anyone has tap-water safe enough to drink in his home.

In the rural areas of Thailand, for example, piped water is available to only 15 per cent of the populace. In rural Pakistan the figure is 11 per cent, and in rural Indonesia, 6 per cent.[6]

Most Asians of necessity draw their water from sources of dubious quality: shallow wells, streams and ponds, canals and ditches, pots of collected rain-water, water vendors.

In the industrialized world, it is automatically assumed that a house has potable water, and few Westerners would dream of living in one that didn't.

The warning "Don't drink the water," with all its fun-poking overtones, applies strictly to the rest of the world.

But to the two-thirds of humanity who have no choice but to "drink the water"—when, that is, they can get any—it is a hardship devoid of much fun.

Besides the inconvenience of having to hand-carry water several times a day from a source often a long trek away, the quality of such water exposes the users to water-related diseases that claim 30,000 lives a day in the developing world.[7]

In an effort to focus global attention on the problem, the 1980s have been internationally designated as "Drinking Water and Sanitation Decade," with the (hopelessly improbable) goal of providing safe drinking water and adequate sanitation to all by 1990.[8]

\* \* \*

The number of those in the world without a fit source of water is being reduced by several million by a long-overdue upgrading of the Bangkok water system which, among its more homey benefits, is enabling Pimol Chame to bathe.

The Thai capital's water system is a relic of its canal-building era. The network of *klongs*, still one of the world's most extensive, once made Bangkok known as "the Venice of the East."

Long after many of the canals have been filled in for streets or building sites, the city's first water-supply canal—dug nearly 75 years ago at the direction of the progressive King Rama V of what was then Siam—still diverts water into Bangkok from the upper reaches of the Chao Phraya River.

This sputtery old system is now being patched up and enlarged with a new water canal and wells, treatment plant, reservoirs, pumping stations, distribution mains, and other facilities costing nearly $1 billion.

More people than the entire population of Laos or New Zealand—4.1 million—will benefit. Some 600,000 of them are obtaining accessible, drinkable water for the first time in their lives. Among them are 150,000 impoverished residents of Bangkok slums.

The rest are gaining better service from a system long so notoriously unreliable.

When water recently began flowing through the new facilities into Thonburi, for thousands of residents it was like being reintroduced to water service all over again.

One of them is a balding, retired naval officer in plaid shorts and plastic sandals named Tanom Yousakul.

He and his family of six live in a little reddish-brown clapboard house, tucked behind an iron fence and a shipboard-tidy front yard on Soi Yingamnuay. For years the house not only got no water in daytime, but never at sufficient pressure to reach the second floor.

His face creases into a smile as he tells of the unaccustomed pleasure of having plenty of water once again.

But old tastes, like old habits, die hard.

While many Bangkokians eagerly use the public water supply for bathing and cooking, they remain reluctant to drink it.

They're wary of the chlorination used to purify it, and repelled by the faint taste of chlorine.

Among them is Pimol Chame. He still collects rainwater for his family to drink. Clay rainwater jugs, fed by a downspout from the roof, line one side of his house—right next to a new public water tap.

# NUKU'ALOFA, TONGA

Tonga adds a new dimension to the word "isolation."

Not so much a country as scattered pieces of a country, it consists of 169 islands strewn across the empty horse-latitudes of the South Pacific Ocean.

Most are fly-specks of coral reefs and palm trees—South Sea "desert islands" minus Dorothy Lamour or ukulele music. Only 36 of them are inhabited.

If skimmed from the sea and assembled shore-to-shore, their combined land area would amount to less than a quarter of the size of the smallest American state, Rhode Island.

But if seascape made a nation, Tonga would be a mega-state. Its wisps of dry land are sprinkled over an expanse of ocean approaching the size of the North Sea.

Some of Tonga's islands lie more than 400 sea-miles from others, with no way of getting there except by boat. Only a few of the larger islands have airstrips.

The nearest continental land mass—Australia—is more than 2,000 miles westward, as the tradewinds blow.

So far away from each other, and from the rest of humanity, Tongans are among the most solitary people on earth. Only now are they becoming linked with their fellow islanders, and with the outside world, by something more immediate than a mail-ship or an occasional airplane.

The telephone—invented more than a century ago—is slowly penetrating remotest Polynesia.

This rural-flavored capital of 20,000 residents (plus unnumbered backyard pigs and chickens) has no television and only a weekly newspaper to put it in touch with the rest of the globe. But it now has a new, direct-dial telephone system.

Radio-telephones link seven other islands, none of which has local telephone service.

The other 28 inhabited islands still lack telecommunications ties of any sort. Plans to install a radio-telephone on each of these islands encounter one complication: all outward calls would have to be "collect," since money isn't used on most of them.

By the standards of Western industrialized countries, where the telephone has become so ubiquitous, this is hardly a telephonic revolution calculated to set Ma Bell to bragging. But it is making a place like Tonga measurably less isolated.

Islanders such as David Hingano remember how difficult it used to be to (in the words of the telephone advertising jingle) "reach out and touch someone."

Before the new telephone exchange was built, if a resident of Tonga's capital wanted to call another, he picked up the phone and waited for an operator—and waited, and waited, often as long as 15 minutes.

"Sometimes you'd go to the exchange yourself to see what the problem was," recalls Mr. Hingano, a government worker with a hearty Polynesian face, dark sarong, and sandals.

Placing a call overseas required even more patience. There were only two lines to the outlying world—high-frequency radio circuits relayed through Fiji, available only during daylight hours on weekdays.

Callers hiked to the post office or to the Department of Telegraphs & Telephones, and waited to be connected. Sometimes it took all day. Others returned home at nightfall without completing their calls.

When a call did go through, Mr. Hingano says, the reception was so faint and crackly with static that it was hard to hear the person on the other end of the line.

Such hardships were happily relegated to history by $3 million worth of new telecommunications equipment, financed by Australia and other international donors.

The new facilities seem to have unloosed within Tongans reservoirs of volubility pent up by centuries of enforced diffidence.

The number of direct-line telephones in the capital has more than tripled in the past decade (from 600 to 2,000). New applications for telephone service arrive every day.

The total time logged in outgoing overseas calls—Tongans can now dial directly to Australia and New Zealand—has more than doubled in just three years.

If this keeps up, it may not only lessen Tongans' remoteness but imperil their reputation as the most reticent of Polynesians.

* * *

Few people in Asia and the Pacific are as physically isolated as Tongans, but most are just about as technologically isolated from modern telecommunications.

As incomprehensible as it may seem to an American or European, the great body of Asians live out their lives without ever talking on a telephone, listening to a radio, or watching a television program.

Even for the relatively few who have had such privileged contact with the electronic age, the likelihood that they possess one of these devices in their homes is remote.

While in North America there is one telephone for every two persons, and in Europe for every three persons, in Asia a telephone serves an average of 35 persons.[1]

Telephone usage is increasing, to be sure. In the past 30 years, the number of telephone subscribers around the world has multiplied more than 10-fold, from 40 million to 550 million. But over three-quarters of them live in the eight leading industrial countries of North America, Western Europe, and Japan.[2]

India, for instance, contains a fifth of humanity but only 0.5 per cent of humanity's telephones (3.1 million). Three out of four of the villages, where 80 per cent of Indians live, have no phone.[3]

Bangladesh, the world's eighth most populous nation, shares each of its telephones (just 122,000 of them) among more than 800 people.[4] Burma, a country with nearly as many people as France (34 million), has only about as many telephones (46,000) as the city of Nice.[5]

Beijing—a city of 9 million and capital of the nation with the largest populace on the globe—has fewer phones (200,000) than Omaha, Nebraska.[6] Shanghai has one phone for every 2,400 people.[7]

The telephone in Asia is almost exclusively a city amenity. In the Philippines, for example, 90 per cent of phones are found in Manila, a city with barely a tenth of the national population.[8]

Becoming a telephone user throughout most of Asia demands liberal investments of both money and patience.

The cost of a private phone is simply beyond the reach of most Asians. In the Philippines, for instance, a residential phone line costs $143 a year—nearly a fifth of the average person's annual income. On top of that, telephone subscribers are required by law to buy $128 worth of stock in the telephone company ($250 for a business phone customer).[9] In Thailand, the cost of acquiring a private line can run as high as $3,000.[10]

Getting a phone connection in most Asian countries entails a wait of several years. In India, it sometimes takes as long as eight years, and in Pakistan, 10 years.[11]

Once the phone is eventually installed, more waiting begins—just to place a call.

Many parts of the continent were introduced to telephone service within a few years of Alexander Graham Bell's revolutionary invention. But much of the equipment being used today remains of nearly as ancient a vintage, such as magneto-powered, manually-operated phone exchanges.

Thais are accustomed to waiting up to 5 minutes in peak periods for a dial tone, and an hour or two to place an international call.[12] Filipinos wait hours to get through to other parts of their own country.[13] Pakistanis manage, on average, to successfully complete only 25 per cent of local calls and 15 per cent of international calls.[14]

Then there's the "wrong number" plague. To own a phone in developing Asia is to very likely receive more of other subscribers' calls than one's own. Much of the fault lies with creaky equipment. In India, 40 per cent of wrong numbers have been determined to result from mechanical failure.[15]

Compared to the telephone, the radio is relatively commonplace. Nearly one Asian in 10 has one. But that's trifling by North American standards. There, radios are almost twice as numerous as people.[16]

Television—an accepted part of the lives of most Westerners—remains an exotic curiosity to most Asians.

One by one, most major Asian governments have invested millions of dollars to introduce television. Thailand was the first on the Asian mainland to do so, back in 1955.[17] Among the most recent were Sri Lanka in 1979, Burma in 1981, and Kampuchea (Cambodia) in 1984.

Two, India and Indonesia, even operate their own television and communication satellites (the latter's launched by the United States). Three others—China, South Korea, and Pakistan—have plans to enter the satellite age.

A scattering of countries in the region remain television virgins. Nepal, which perhaps is still too busy listening to its first modern radio station (opened in 1983), is one. Bhutan, Laos, Papua New Guinea, and most of the Pacific island states also are yet without television service.

Most Asian television systems broadcast a few hours a day to a relative handful of city viewers. Barely three out of every 100 Asians have television sets.[18] They are confined mostly to the small urban minorities of these heavily agrarian societies.

In India, only 9,000 of the country's 580,000 villages have television sets—communal ones—more than half of which are in disrepair at any given time.[19]

In Indonesia, three-quarters of adults in Jakarta are said to own television sets, while in the nation as a whole less than one person in 100 does so.[20] The new Sri Lankan television system reaches just 30 miles beyond the capital city of Colombo.[21] Burmese television began transmitting outside the capital, Rangoon, only in 1983.[22]

Home television remains the entertainment of the rich. A color television set in China, for example, costs the average person the equivalent of two years' income.[23] In India, a black-and-white set — color was introduced only in 1982 — soaks up a year's income.[24]

The penetration of Asia's developing countries by telecommunications is even more modest than the regional statistics would indicate, since they are inflated by the inclusion of electronically-advanced Japan and fast-modernizing city-states like Hong Kong and Singapore.

In Japan — the home of Sony, Hitachi, and Panasonic — a near-saturation 99.2 per cent of households own color television sets.[25]

A television set in China, by contrast, is stretched among 67 people. In places such as India and Bangladesh, the prevalence drops to the order of one set for every several hundred persons.[26]

The favored owners of Bangladesh's 260,000 TV sets watch canned American re-runs of "Dallas," "Six Million Dollar Man," and "Knight Rider,"[27] while the other 99 million Bangladeshis watch candlelight flicker on the dingy mud walls of their huts.

In Asia, at least, the "wired village" so optimistically envisioned by futurists still seems very distant.

## KATHMANDU, NEPAL

The business of His Majesty's Government here is conducted on the most unregal-looking bundles of papers.

Dog-eared and limp from handling by a thousand official fingers, they are toggled together by soiled ribbons or worn metal clasps.

Rarely do these government files receive anything so extravagant as a new entry typewritten on a separate sheet of paper.

Most updating is squeezed economically in longhand (with official seals and signatures) into any blank space that might remain on the original document.

Nepal is one nation that does not have a bureaucracy which generates much paperwork, for the simple reason that it does not have much paper.

This Himalayan kingdom of 16 million people consumes the least amount of paper, per person, of any country in Asia for which figures are available.

It has (as of this writing) no paper mill. Every scrap of manufactured paper is a foreign import, expensive and sporadically supplied.

* * *

In the Western industrialized world, the humble slip of paper ranks as just about the most ordinary, throwaway item ever to be taken for granted. But

51

in developing Asia—not just Nepal, but most of the region's poorer nations—paper is a scarce commodity, often bordering on luxury.

Paper is by no means the only such product, or even the most important. But a closer look at Asia's paper shortage may shed a few insights into the many items, so commonly accepted by Westerners, whose sparseness in much of the rest of the world makes everyday life more difficult.

In his use of paper, the average Nepali is a model of wasteless rectitude. For every sheet of paper which he consumes, the average American consumes a ream.

Most fellow Asians are only slightly less abstemious, as can be seen in the following comparison of per capita consumption of paper in selected countries during one recent year (1980).

| | |
|---|---|
| Nepal | 1.1 pounds |
| Bangladesh | 1.2 |
| India | 5.9 |
| Indonesia | 6.3 |
| China | 20.9 |
| Singapore | 209.9 |
| Japan | 294.8 |
| United States | 600.6 |

*Source:* Asian Development Bank, *Appraisal Report, Paper Mill Technical Services Project (Nepal),* December 1982.

Among 15 countries encompassing most of developing Asia, the consumption figure averages about 31 pounds—dropping to only about 18 pounds if fast-industrializing Singapore is excluded.[1]

While the spectacle of government bureaucrats being deprived of paper may strike some as a positive blessing, in other spheres the region's paper shortage creates undeniable hardships.

One place pinched the hardest is schools. It's a rare classroom anywhere in developing Asia that has an adequate supply of textbooks, writing paper, and other paper instructional materials.

In China, the dearth of textbooks is a chronic complaint of students.[2] In India, even heavy government subsidies leave vast numbers of schoolchildren without textbooks. In Pakistan—which, like Nepal, produces little of its own paper or printing—students are compelled to resort to pirated copies of textbooks to try and fill the gap.[3]

The textbook shortage has corrupted universities, throughout Asia's developing regions, into mere memorization factories. Students read little besides their lecture notes. Libraries, pitiably understocked, serve mainly as study halls where students commit to memory the notes from their class lectures—often obligingly delivered at dictation speed.[4]

Economist Gunnar Myrdal, in his landmark study of South and Southeast Asia, concluded that "the most serious deficiency hampering educational efforts is the scarcity of paper for writing and for printing books and other educational material."[5]

Books other than textbooks also are left in short supply.

Most Asians, in fact, probably never see a book published in their own language. Asia and other parts of the Third World publish only about one out of every 10 books issued worldwide every year. The rest are published by the one-quarter of the earth's people who live in the industrialized nations—predominantly in one of five European languages.

India, for example, manages to keep available in print only about 13,000 book titles—less than 2 per cent of the number of *new* titles published globally in a single year.[6]

Pakistan operates just 600 libraries for its nearly 100 million inhabitants (compared, for instance, with New York City's 200 public libraries for a population of 7 million). The 3.5 million books on their shelves (half as many as the main New York City library) amount to only one book for every 63 Pakistanis. And 350 towns have no library at all.[7]

Limited availability of paper isn't the only constraint, of course, in an Asian book-reading market narrowed by widespread poverty and illiteracy. But it is an important factor in preventing the supply of books from meeting even the modest existing demand.

In China, where the paper shortage is severe, book publishers squabble openly over scanty supplies. The popular "pulp" press is accused by those who publish more-serious works of gobbling up too big a share of the precious commodity.[8]

Inadequate quantities of one of the cheapest types of paper—newsprint—meanwhile, hamper Asian newspapers in their important role of disseminating mass information.

Newspapers in the industrialized world devour newsprint with gluttonous abandon. Those in the United States, serving barely 5 per cent of the world's population, swallow up nearly 40 per cent of the globe's entire annual production of newsprint.[9]

A single copy of the Sunday edition of *The New York Times* uses as much newsprint as several months' issues of most papers in developing Asia.

The press in this region is permitted no such profligacy.

Dailies in the world's most populous country—China—are normally restricted in size to between 8 and 16 pages, in large measure because of the low stocks and high costs of newsprint. And the cramped, space-saving formats hardly encourage readership.[10]

In the second-largest nation, India, the supply of newsprint imposes a similar restraint on the press. It consumes as much as one-half of newspaper production costs, and is rationed by the government.

Over half of the country's newsprint is imported. Although India produces much of its own newsprint, ironically, the local output is not only inferior in quality but also twice as expensive as imported newsprint.

With newspaper circulation growing faster than domestic production of newsprint—annual consumption is forecast to double by the end of the century—India's reliance on imported newsprint is expected to increase. Government reluctance to substantially boost imports of newsprint, many fear, may force newspapers to become smaller or publish less frequently.[11]

Asia's third-biggest country, Indonesia, manufactures not a column-inch of its own newsprint. To curb the demand of its whirring presses, the government limits all newspapers to 12 pages and advertising space to 35 per cent of total content.[12]

The relative paucity of all manner of reading and writing materials in developing Asia, due to the shortage of paper, is hard not only on readers and writers. It undercuts basic literacy.

With nothing to read or write on, millions who achieve nominal literacy never reach functional literacy or else relapse into illiteracy. It is estimated that two-thirds of those who learn to read and write every year eventually lose this ability.[13]

* * *

No country is more aware of the privations of being paper-poor, perhaps, than Nepal. But relief is on the way. The continent's most sparing consumer of paper is about to get its own paper industry.

Until now, the only paper produced in the country has been a negligible amount made by rural families by hand from the inner bark of the *lokta* plant found (in diminishing quantities) on some foothills of the Himalayas.

Even in this nation accustomed to doing without paper, consumption is increasing at a rate of 16 per cent a year. To satisfy its growing appetite, Nepal imports some 8,000 tons a year, mostly from India to the south, at a cost of $8 million. Besides the high price, shipments encounter frequent delays.

Matters may improve with the completion of no fewer than three paper mills now being planned or built. One is being erected by Nepal's northern neighbors, the Chinese, while another is a government enterprise, and the third private.

Since Nepal has precious few remaining forests for pulp, all three new mills will produce their paper from local fibrous plants: straw from rice and wheat, and *sabai* grass.

Unlike pulpwood, both of these papermaking ingredients are happily abundant here. Surplus straw is discarded by farmers, and the grass—a tough inhabitant of the southern slopes of the Siwalik mountain ranges—is spurned by cattle.

By the end of the decade, the new mills are projected to be supplying three-quarters of the country's demand for paper.[14]

Nepal will remain a long way from the modern paper-glutted society of triplicate copies, over-packaging, and litterbugs—mercifully—but the common piece of paper should become a little more common.

# Everyday Energy
# and Environmental Crises

## BRAHMANBARIA, BANGLADESH

There is nothing in the appearance of Mohammed Siddqur Rahman to mark him as a cultural pioneer.

A vehicle driver for a government agency, he is self-effacingly polite and indefinably middle-aged. Like so many Bangladeshis, he bears the rigors of life in this impoverished country with a stoical dignity.

But when Mr. Siddqur goes home to a supper of curry and rice, he dines in trend-setting style. His meal is cooked on a gas stove.

A gas-cooked dinner might be nothing special in Baltimore, or Brussels, or Brisbane. But in Bangladesh, it sets Mr. Siddqur sharply apart from centuries of ancestors and most of his contemporaries.

For at least 2,000 years, firewood has been the predominant household fuel here on the Indian subcontinent — as, indeed, throughout much of the nonindustrialized world. And it still is.[1]

In Bangladesh, for example, over two-thirds of energy consumption comes from firewood, supplemented by other age-old sources such as straw, rice husks, jute stems, and dried cow-dung.[2] But with the population mounting and the forests shrinking (only 8 per cent of the country is now under tropical forests), fuelwood grows increasingly scarce.[3]

Families must trudge farther and scour longer for wood. Gathering one day's supply of firewood for an average Bangladeshi family of five is now estimated to take the equivalent of a full day's work by one family member.[4]

Like millions of others here, Mr. Siddqur used to find himself increasingly resorting to kerosene. But for dirt-poor Bangladeshis, kerosene is onerously expensive. Every drop must be imported.

Hence the liberating impact of something as seemingly insignificant as a household gas connection is hard to overestimate.

Mr. Siddqur and his fellow Bangladeshis—woefully shortchanged in almost all of the world's natural resources—are amply endowed in one: natural gas.

A string of 10 gas fields, stretching from the Bay of Bengal northward across the eastern side of the country, give the nation enough proven reserves of gas to last 200 years at current, very-low consumption rates.[5]

It's Bangladesh's only exploitable indigenous energy source, and it's being rapidly tapped.

The gas that cooks Mr. Siddqur's curry comes from a cluster of wells just north of here known as the Titas field—one of the country's four producing fields.

When the gas main came tunneling toward their house two and a half years ago, Mr. Siddqur and his wife saw an opportunity to stop having to scrounge for firewood or buy expensive kerosene.

He bought a one-burner gas stove for 200 taka (about $10), scraped together 2,000 taka ($100) for the connection fee, and now pays 22 taka ($1.10) per month for gas service.

"It's cheaper than kerosene," he tells a visitor in Bengali. "And my wife finds it easier for cooking."

Some 4,000 other residents of Brahmanbaria have now hooked up to gas. Another 135,000 households in Dhaka, the capital city 60 miles to the southwest, are piped gas from the Titas field. It also fuels two fertilizer factories and a power plant.

* * *

A country like Bangladesh—one of the world's least developed—consumes relatively little petroleum. With nearly half as many people as the United States, it uses only about as much oil as a large American city.*

But consumption is increasing, and oil now ranks as the main commercial fuel. The cost, for this destitute country, is proportionately much higher than for more-prosperous countries.

It's a predicament in which Bangladesh is, alas, far from alone.

In Asia, all but a handful of developing countries—ranging from giant

---

* Three million tons of oil equivalent in fiscal year 1981 (total commercial energy consumption), of which about one-half was imported oil and oil products (according to *Asian Electric Power Utilities Data Book* [Manila: Asian Development Bank, 1983], p. 25). This is less than consumed by, for example, the San Francisco metropolitan area.

India to tiny South Pacific atolls—rely on imported oil for 70 per cent or more of their commercial energy needs.

The financial drain is sapping the strength of frail economies. After more than a decade of adjusting to higher oil prices, a survey by the Asian Development Bank finds that low-income countries still spend half of their annual export earnings to import oil.

For the poorest of the poor, the diversion of financial resources approaches a flood. Bangladesh, for example, was expected to pay over 90 per cent of its export earnings for oil in 1985—and by 1990 to pay every taka of them, and more besides.[6]

What's a poor country to do?

One answer is to replace imported oil by exploiting, to the extent that it can, whatever indigenous energy resources it might have.

That's a tall order, of course, demanding heavy doses of money, expertise, and ingenuity. And some countries are clearly better fitted than others to do so.

But even the least-endowed nation possesses some native energy potential, whether it's mountain streams that could be harnessed for hydropower or livestock herds whose waste could be decomposed into biogas.

Driven by economic necessity, nearly all Asian countries are making efforts to wean themselves from oil. Other examples, both large and small:

## SRI LANKA

Nestled in the creases of the crinkly mountain spine of this island nation, adrift off the tip of India, are scores of small, white-painted factories.

They are dwarfed by the steep slopes rising on all sides, terraced from top to bottom with low, shimmery bushes as if swathed in green corduroy—tea.

It's in these factories that the small, green leaves plucked from those bushes are transformed into powdery, black, pungent Ceylon tea savored by millions of tea drinkers around the world.

To fire the heaters that wither and dry the tea leaves, most of the factories burn petroleum fuel. In a poor country totally dependent on imported oil whose price has skyrocketed in recent years, such fuel has become uneconomically expensive.

A solution is suggested by the few tea factories that don't fuel their heaters with petroleum. They burn, instead, wood. The wood does the job just as well, and costs much less money.

Soon more tea factories will be burning wood. Fifteen factories are to be converted from oil (three others already use wood) as part of a rehabilitation of declining tea estates in the Badulla area of central Sri Lanka.

Fast-growing species of trees will be planted on 4,300 acres of nearby land that is unsuitable for tea, unused, or wasteground, to provide a continual supply of fuelwood.

The switch from oil to wood is expected to save half a million dollars a year.

The oil-import-cutting project is partially financed by—ironically enough—the world's oil-exporting countries, through the OPEC Fund for International Development.

## FIJI

The tourists' Fiji—the gleaming beaches and five-star hotels—is left behind.

Then agricultural Fiji—coastal sugar cane fields and narrow-gauge sugar-mill railways—disappears in the distance.

Climbing into the interior foothills of Viti Levu, Fiji's main island, cultivation gives way to rain forest.

Neat country cottages are roofed in steeply-sloped thatch, the ridge beam (or *bure*) protruding distinctively at each gable.

Wild boars are hunted by boys with spears.

The gravel road twists higher, toward toothy volcanic peaks poking 12,000 feet into the sky.

These craggy highlands were, until recently, virtually without either roads or people. It's easy to understand why.

Up here, the cheery South Pacific sun is a rare visitor. Cold, soaking mists envelop most days, giving a perpetual sheen to the dark rock and nurturing lush stands of virgin pine.

Yet this inhospitable site offers something that may be more valuable to Fiji than tourism or sugar, the two pillars of the country's economy: independence from imported oil for power.

Small island nations such as Fiji and its Pacific neighbors are among the world's most import-reliant. Like most of them, Fiji imports nearly all of its fuel for generating electricity, at a crippling economic cost.

A country with fewer people than the city of San Diego, California (about 670,000), Fiji has been paying $1.5 million a month for diesel oil for its power plants. That's nearly half of the money it earns from its exports.

In some other South Pacific nations, the oil bill soaks up all the export earnings—or even more. The financial burden typically raises the cost of goods and services in Oceania by anywhere from 10 to 40 per cent.[7]

For Fiji, a means of escape lies in its intimidating interior.

The very features that have always made the area so repellant to most people—its highness and wetness—make it attractive for hydroelectric power.

Now taking shape here is a hydropower project which, in terms of relative cost and economic impact, looms as important to Fiji as the Tennessee Valley Authority project in the United States or the Aswan Dam in Egypt.

A 221-feet-high dam has transformed an obscure stream called Nanuku Creek into a reservoir lake winding 10 miles back into the mountains. The water plunges through more than 3 miles of tunnels, bored mostly through solid rock, to spin four 20-megawatt turbines in a powerhouse in the valley below.

The Monasavu project has brought to this austere setting an oddly cosmopolitan atmosphere.

The financing is broadly international, with loans from four of the world's multilateral lending institutions.

The work force—numbering 1,500 at the project's height—blends engineers from Britain, Switzerland, Australia, and New Zealand with local workers from the country's own melting-pot of ethnic Fijians, Indians, and Chinese.

The cost of the Monasavu project is hefty: an estimated $220 million, or roughly a fifth of the country's entire annual economic output. But the dividends, too, will be immense.

When completed, it will supply all of the island's electrical needs, except for one area too small and remote to connect.

And there will be ample capacity for growth. The 35 per cent of Fijians who now have electricity is increasing at the rate of 5,000 new customers a year.

Construction has been underway since 1978, and the main power plant was commissioned in 1983.

Far below, in the seaside capital city of Suva—a bouncy, three-hour trip by Land-Rover—the Monasavu project is already tangibly improving electrical service.

At a cement factory that ranks as the country's biggest power consumer, officials of Fiji Industries Ltd. welcome the end of the daily blackouts which disrupted their operations a few years ago.

The blackouts, triggered by breakdowns in the aging, diesel-fired power system, regularly ground the plant to a halt.

"We used to have to shut down for at least an hour and a half every day," says a company electrical engineer.

With annual sales of $8 million and a payroll of 176 employees, the shutdowns carried national economic repercussions.

At another of Fiji's major employers and electricity users—the country's only brewery—officials voice relief over the easing of another old problem: power surges.

Voltage fluctuations frequently ruined equipment at the Suva plant of Carlton Brewery (Fiji) Ltd., which provides the country with 100 jobs and 4.3 million gallons of beer a year.

Few Fijians who sip a pint of beer, or buy a bag of cement—or switch on a light—probably have more than the vaguest idea where Monasavu is, or what's being built there.

Yet those cloud-veiled heights offer them a bright promise of energy self-reliance.

## PAKISTAN

Defying the mapmakers, this Asian country often seems firmly rooted in the Middle East.

In Karachi, Pakistan's largest city, a sprawl of dusty concrete amid undulating desert, motor vehicles share the roads with carts drawn by trudging camels.

Bazaars, much like those in Cairo or Baghdad, teem with men draped in the traditional *shalwar-qamiz*—shirts flowing to mid-thigh over billowy trousers.

Urdu, the national language, borrows heavily from Arabic and Persian, and is written in the same squiggly script.

But Pakistan is most un-Middle Eastern in one unfortunate respect: it has no oil sheiks, no petrodollar riches, and practically no oil of its own.

It must import 90 per cent of the oil it consumes, a costly necessity which lumps it squarely into the company of most of the world's poor, developing countries.

One of the most heavily-populated, low-income countries—its 96 million people each earn the average equivalent of $1 a day—Pakistan nevertheless has managed something to be envied by many a rich nation. While importing nearly all of its oil, it has become two-thirds self-sufficient in energy.

Pakistan is a long way from losing its thirst for imported oil, still a $900-million-a-year habit. But it seems to have shaken primary dependence on the fuel.

This achievement has been made possible chiefly by developing the country's prime domestic energy asset: natural gas.

The plains astride the lower stretches of the Indus River are bubbled with gas fields, which now supply over 40 per cent of Pakistan's energy requirements and meet a steady increase in consumption at the rate of more than 8 per cent a year.

Some 87 per cent of the country's gas supply comes from the Sui field, one of the world's largest known gas deposits, 300 miles north of Karachi.

Gas from Sui and several smaller fields now fuels nearly 1,000 industrial plants, 7,700 commercial establishments, and 400,000 homes. As a substitute for imported oil, it saves the country an estimated 10 billion rupees ($800 million) a year—almost halving the annual oil bill which it would otherwise have to pay.[8]

The benefits ripple across the Pakistan economy.

One important new industry has sprung up largely due to the availability of gas: steelmaking.

A few years ago, the industry didn't exist. Pakistan imported all of its iron and steel requirements, at a cost in 1981 of $162 million. Lacking the raw materials that seemed necessary—iron ore, adequate coal, or fuel oil—it had little choice.

The economic equation changed dramatically, however, with the tapping of the country's gas reserves.

A massive, $2 billion steelworks is now rising on a 25-square-mile site east of Karachi. It lies at the end of a 16-inch gas main that fuels its blast furnaces, coke oven, and electrical generators.

At full operation, the Pakistan Steel mill is expected to employ 15,000 workers and make the nation self-sufficient in steel.

Gas also lights up Karachi—or at least the one-quarter of its households that have electricity. All is gas-generated.

At one of the two generating stations on the city's fringes, four 25-megawatt turbine units herald nightfall with a deafening hum as they pump power toward the metropolis, silhouetted against the sunset-reddened horizon.

The engineer in charge, a trimly-moustached young man named Salim Sanjar, says firing the generators with gas is 10 times cheaper than with oil.

In its endowment with gas as an alternative to imported oil, Pakistan is fortunate—but by no means alone.

At least 10 other Asian developing countries are reckoned by the Asian Development Bank's energy survey as likely to have substantial, yet-to-be-developed gas deposits.

They include Afghanistan, Bangladesh, the Indochina countries, and Papua New Guinea—some of the most energy-strapped nations on earth.[9]

## TONGA

Not all attempts to replace imported oil with a local substitute, however, work.

One such promising idea that didn't quite live up to expectations is found here, on a hilltop commanding a South Pacific panorama capable of inspiring anyone to indulge in a bit of dreaming.

Amid the monotonous coral flatness of Tonga's main island, the Malai'eua hill rates as something of a natural wonder. It rises just 85 feet, but its summit of stately coconut palms and waist-deep grass looks out upon a turquoise lagoon and the green clump of rugged 'Eua Island beyond.

More important to the residents of this island, lacking either a lake or stream, the hill is a kind of waterworks. It contains the island's source of drinking water.

But the pumps that draw it from wells, and feed it into the municipal water-supply system for the capital of Nuku'alofa, are fueled by diesel oil and oil-generated electricity. The 24 pumps guzzle 400 gallons of oil a month.

When oil began soaring in cost, someone had an ingenious idea. Noticing that the Malai'eua heights seemed well ventilated by Pacific breezes, why not pump the water by wind-power?

The Tonga government got a loan from the Asian Development Bank in Manila to test the idea by erecting three 45-feet-high windmills. For a year and a half, the windmills competed with the diesel and electric pumps. The windmills lost.

Each windmill pumped, on average, only about a fourth as much water as an electric pump and a fifth as much as a diesel pump. The windmills were twice as expensive to operate as electric pumps, per gallon of water pumped, and nearly three times as expensive as diesel pumps.[10]

The hitch: too little wind, especially at night.

The foreman who tends the pumps, a white-haired, grandfatherly mechanic named Seti Finau, says there is enough wind to generate top windmill production only in one day out of every 10.

The other problem, paradoxically, is too much wind. The windmills have proven highly vulnerable to damage by hurricanes. When Hurricane Isaac roared across the island in 1982, it put the windmills out of commission for four months.

So much for this bold venture in indigenous and renewable energy. Perhaps it had to be tried—if nothing else, to show that it wouldn't work.

## KATHMANDU, NEPAL

Here in her stone-floored kitchen, Rupa Joshi knew what it meant to live in one of the world's poorest countries.

There were four generations of family under her roof to be fed from this kitchen, but no reliable source of cooking fuel.

Bottled butane gas often was unavailable because of a shortage of cylinders. Kerosene was too expensive. Electricity was prone to sudden interruptions, sometimes amid meal preparation. Firewood—of which she tucked away a small stock as a last resort—was growing increasingly scarce.

Repeated in the kitchens of hundreds of thousands of households in this fuel-starved Himalayan kingdom, Mrs. Joshi's problem is one of national proportions.

Much to her relief, she recently got her reliable source of cooking fuel— but not in the big, high-technology, macro-economic way in which such problems usually are tackled. No hydroelectric dam was built, no power plant erected, no gas field developed.

Mrs. Joshi's new cooking fuel comes, quite literally, from her back yard.

Here on the fringes of Kathmandu, where the capital's clutter of ancient pagodas, noisy markets, and little wooden-balconied houses gives way to lush rice terraces and muddy dirt roads, the Joshi family is making its own "biogas."

The seven milk cows kept behind the house supply the raw material. Their dung, mixed with water, is fed into a cement dome buried in the ground. The slurry decomposes into methane gas, which is piped to a burner in the kitchen.

The beneficiary of this ingenious little operation is a dark-eyed, young mother of two. Mrs. Joshi's long black hair is gathered at the back and draped over one shoulder of her curry-colored sari. A tiny *nakpaul* ring adorns one nostril and an assortment of bangles jingle on her wrists.

She smiles shyly when asked her opinion of the new fuel. But her reply is unequivocal. Biogas, she avers, is not only utterly reliable but half as expensive as bottled gas.

\* \* \*

Not so long ago, the agencies involved in developing impoverished countries like Nepal would not have bothered themselves with Mrs. Joshi's cooking fuel.

With the needs so staggering, development tended to be viewed on a grander scale. There were ports to be built, highways, water systems, irrigation schemes, mines, factories, electrification.

The projects were big. They were technically complex. And they often introduced radically different ways of doing things.

These large-scale facilities are still needed and still being built. But a new appreciation is now dawning for concepts once all but scorned: smallness, simplicity, and tradition.

Human-scale and human-level assistance projects, it is found, are sometimes the most cost-effective, most easily assimilated, and only practical way of improving conditions.

The idea of putting small biogas units in the back yards of Nepal families like the Joshis got a nudge after a Nepali development official traveled to the English Midlands town of Rugby a few years ago to participate in a program conducted by Intermediate Technology Industrial Services, founded by the late E. F. Schumacher, an economist who wrote the book *Small Is Beautiful*.[1]

The visitor, a trim, precise man named G. R. Shrestha of the Agricultural Development Bank of Nepal, returned from Rugby as an apostle of appropriately-scaled technology.

The government-run bank where Mr. Shrestha works has almost single-handedly brought biogas to Nepal.

It helped establish a company in 1977 to manufacture biogas equipment. And its low-interest loans have financed most of the 1,200 units installed in the country since then.

The loans are essential because even a small, family-size model is expensive by Nepal standards: about $770 — a price-tag which the company is striving hard to reduce. Despite the cost, the number of units is expected to triple in two years.

The 2,000 new biogas units alone are projected to save Nepal 150,000 gallons of kerosene and 10,000 tons of fuelwood, while saving the families who own them between $100 and $900 a year, depending on the size of their unit. Use of the leftover slurry as fertilizer will enrich the soil with an estimated 1,400 tons of plant nutrients.

Biogas is becoming almost commonplace in several other Asian countries. India and Pakistan each have about 100,000 biogas units. China, the leader in this field, has 7 million.[2]

* * *

Other evidence of a growing recognition that bigness, complexity, and modernity are not necessarily better is found elsewhere in Nepal and other parts of the continent.

Come visit, for instance, the little town of Malekhu, nestled in the scrubby foothills of the Himalayas 40 miles west of Kathmandu.

A lane of lumpy clay, worn rock-hard by the padding of centuries of sandals, twists from the main Kathmandu-Pokhara road downward to a river. It is lined with blocky little two-story buildings, managing somehow to look at the same time both sturdy and frail. Some are built of whitewashed stone and others of wood, many with heavy-timbered balconies weathered grey.

The open fronts contain shops—a few sparsely-stocked general stores, a grain dealer (heaps of bags encroaching on the lane), rustic eating establishments. In one, the proprietor is frying round potato cakes in a long-handled pan on a wood stove of baked mud.

At one end of the lane, a group of local women—a palette of color in their saris of blue, green, and pink, beribboned hair, and shiny metal bracelets—squat in a semicircle with brass pots, waiting their turn to draw water from a communal pump.

The wonders of electricity arrived here in Malekhu two years ago. Electricity now helps local farmers to more efficiently hull their rice, grind their flour, and crush their mustard seed. A couple of fluorescent tube lights illuminate the outdoor market in the evening. Lightbulbs will soon be introduced into 20 homes.

As power projects go, this one is puny and rudimentary. Water diverted from the river runs a 15-horsepower turbine no larger than a sewing machine, which, in turn, powers various crop-processing machinery and a 12-kilowatt generator.

The whole setup is uncomplicated enough to be operated quite satisfactorily by a local ex-farmer named Pancha Krishna Shrestha. (He's no relation to the biogas proponent; the name is as common in Nepal as Smith in the United States.)

Neither Mr. Shrestha nor the little town of Malekhu need—or want—anything more elaborate.

Throughout developing Asia, such small plants are the big growth area in hydropower technology.

Tens of thousands of "mini-" and "micro-" hydro plants have been built on countless small rivers and streams. China alone has installed more than 90,000 of them.[3]

* * *

Traditional practices, too, seem to be commanding new respect.

Firewood is an example.

As the Third World's forests are systematically stripped away, billions of dollars have been spent developing alternatives to firewood, such as electricity and natural gas. The effort has frequently yielded diminishing returns, however, in reaching the distant, often remote villages where most people in these countries live.

Increasingly—as we'll see in a later chapter—development agencies are opting to help the rural poor to continue burning firewood, instead of trying to switch them from it.

Forests are being planted, not, as in the past, to produce commercial timber, but to provide renewable supplies of firewood for local residents.[4]

* * *

Tradition is being honored even more scrupulously in another corner of Asia where tradition is practically a way of life: the mystical Indonesian island of Bali.

Agricultural life on this volcano-studded island has been organized with cunning efficiency for 1,000 years or longer. The water that courses down the mountains is gathered in gravity-defying canals and tunnels, and then fed to networks of irrigated rice terraces. The precious fluid is apportioned among farmers through ancient water associations called *subaks*.

A few years ago, international development agencies were brought in to try to improve crop production and rural living conditions. Their experts reexamined everything according to the most up-to-date agricultural concepts.

This is often the prelude to an entirely new irrigation system, or at least a sweeping overhaul of existing methods. But in this case, it wasn't. The experts decided they could improve little on the basic system which the Balinese had been operating for centuries. It needed only a bit of upgrading.

Working closely with the farmers' *subaks*, two projects financed by the European Economic Community and the Asian Development Bank are rehabilitating and refining 67 small irrigation facilities across the island. Masonry dams, for example, are replacing those of boulders and bamboo often breached by storms.

A group of *subak* members chat about their experience on the porch of the village office in the village of Buahan. Banana and coffee plants nod in the breeze just outside, and pigs are squealing somewhere beyond.

Across the road can be glimpsed the black-thatched roof of one of the thousands of small temples that give this island an empyreal air.

The elected chief of these farmers' *subak* is a small, spare man with thinning black hair, his leather-sandaled feet tucked under him on the rung of a steel folding chair. His first name—the full name is Wayan Mugereg—indicates that he is the eldest son in his family.

Like the others, he is pleased, although not surprised, that their ancient irrigation system withstood foreign scrutiny. "It is very simple," he says, "but designed well."

## SEOUL, SOUTH KOREA

Korea may be "the Land of the Morning Calm," but not, alas, here.

Orange dump trucks rumble in from all directions, disgorging loads of garbage that raise ever higher the mountains of trash in an eerie moonscape of rubbish, dust, smoke, stench, scavengers, shacks, and flies.

On one side, beyond the mounds and fumes, can be glimpsed the smart new office and apartment buildings of the booming Korean capital.

On the other side flows the broad expanse of the Han River, the country's largest, its banks lined with plots of green vegetables.

This is Nanjido, the 700-acre dump that absorbs nearly 23,000 tons a day of household wastes generated by Seoul's 10 million residents.

Cleaning up behind one of the world's fastest growing and most crowded city populations is a major undertaking. It occupies 800 garbage-collection vehicles and an estimated 10,000 people, including dump pickers.

But it also spawns serious pollution problems.

Open burning at the Nanjido dump befouls air that already ranks (in its high content of dust and sulphur dioxide) among the most polluted of major cities of the world.

Seepage from the dump is believed to be contaminating ground water. The adjoining Han River, which supplies most of Seoul's drinking water, already is badly polluted.

What's more, Nanjido—blanketed with rubbish averaging 20 feet deep after seven years of dumping—will soon be filled to capacity, forcing the city to find an alternative.

* * *

Seoul's giant dump, and its giant problems, epitomize the environmental challenge facing Korea as a whole.

For most of the past 25 years, the country was too busy achieving its celebrated "economic miracle" to heed the resulting impact on its natural habitat.

During that period, economic output has grown 20-fold,[1] and Korea has become a world-class industrial power in several fields. A nation once predominantly rural has been transformed, meanwhile, into one largely urban. Abandoning the countryside at the rate of half a million a year, more than three-quarters of Koreans now live in cities. Seoul itself has quintupled in population.[2]

But the environmental cost of these dizzying changes has been heavy.

The tonnage of pollutants discharged into Korea's air every year is reckoned by the government to have nearly tripled since the mid-1960s. On many winter days, with fumes spewing from millions of traditional *ondol* coal heaters, Seoul is enveloped in thick, acrid smog.[3]

Rivers and coastal waters suffer from a lag in modern waste disposal facilities. Sewers serve only 70 per cent of urban residents and virtually no rural dwellers. Up-to-date sewage treatment plants operate just in the two largest cities of Seoul and Busan, handling in the Korean capital a scant 8 per cent of the sewage.

Only half of the country's residents are provided collection services for garbage and rubbish, most of it winding up in dumps like Nanjido.[4]

\* \* \*

The deterioration of Korea's environment is, unfortunately, far from unique. It is occurring in country after country throughout developing Asia. Consider:

- Asia's overcrowded cities contain some of the most polluted air in the world. Residents of Shanghai, for example, breathe air that is 10 times more contaminated than American standards allow.[5] Bangkok's air is tainted with twice as much carbon monoxide as that of Washington, D.C.[6]
- The burdens of high population and a low level of sanitary sewage disposal impose an increasing strain on Asian rivers and seas. Bombay dumps more than 300 million gallons a day of untreated industrial wastewater into the Arabian Sea.[7] Jakarta Bay contains lethal quantities of metal pollution.[8] Once-scenic Manila Bay is unfit for swimming.
- Many Asian cities sometimes seem in danger of choking in their own trash. Calcutta, for instance, generates 2,500 tons of garbage a day, and Bombay, 3,500 tons, much of which is simply left to packs of stray dogs and rats that outnumber the human residents.[9]
- Soil erosion is sapping the fertility of half a million square miles of land in

South Asia and China alone, according to the United Nations Environment Program. The Ganges River carries away an average of 1.4 billion tons of sediment a year; the Brahmaputra, 750 million tons; the Indus, 440 million tons; and the Mekong, 170 million tons.[10]

• Asian tropical forests are shrinking at an estimated rate of 2 per cent a year, threatening to lose the region 70 per cent of its forest cover by the end of the century.[11]

\* \* \*

Long dismissed as a "rich man's problem," irrelevant to poor, developing countries, environmental protection is arousing growing (if belated) concern among Asian governments.

Antipollution programs, virtually nonexistent a decade ago, have been launched by at least 16 Asian countries and 23 Pacific island nations and territories.

China has elevated ecological concern to the vice-premier level, with an unprecedented (and unprecedentedly candid) "state of the environment" speech in 1984 by Vice-Premier Li Peng. The country has established an environmental policing agency empowered to penalize polluters. And it is earmarking 7 per cent of its industrial-development budget for antipollution technology.[12]

Indonesia has a cabinet minister charged with overseeing population growth and the environment.[13]

India has a Department of Environment, and bold plans to (among other things) clean up the Ganges, the holiest—and one of the filthiest—of the country's rivers.[14]

New factories and other development projects are subjected to American-style environmental impact assessments (of varying effectiveness) in India, Malaysia, the Philippines, and Thailand.[15]

Even the poor (but environmentally rich) Himalayan kingdom of Nepal, too strapped to do much on its own, has formed a nature conservation trust under the sponsorship of the king to raise funds for environmental protection—chiefly from international donors.[16]

But the surest sign of a maturing sensitivity may be the rise of a form of grassroots expression rather new to developing Asia: citizen environmental action groups.

The Korea Antipollution Organization is a vocal watchdog here. Others have sprung up from India to the Pacific atolls.

One citizen activist, Gurmit Singh, president of the Environmental Protection Society of Malaysia, claims that "Asians are gradually becoming more critical of the development being thrust on them."

"Even the poor," he says, "are not willing to accept a poisoned loaf."[17]

Perhaps because its level of contamination is so serious, Korea has been among the cleanup leaders. As industrialization and urbanization intensified in the late 1970s, a dawning public awareness of the accompanying pollution led to enactment in 1977 of a landmark environmental quality law.[18]

The Office of Environment, created to implement the law, now fields a staff of 390 across the country.

Dr. In-Hwan Kim, an American-educated economist who directs the agency's planning, has watched with interest the change in Korean attitudes toward environmental protection.

"Ten years ago, everybody in the government sector was scared of talking about pollution because they felt the first priority was economic development, regardless of the environmental result," he says.

"But now, even people who are economic-development-minded realize that we can't wait any longer—we must invest some of the fruits of industrial development to protect the environment."

This new concern is well illustrated by an ambitious cleanup plan for the Han River basin.

No area of the country, perhaps, is more environmentally important. The basin through which the Han River wends its way to the Yellow Sea is home to nearly one-third of South Koreans (11.6 million), two of their four largest cities (Seoul and Incheon) as well as 32 other communities, and more than 8,000 industries.

The river carries roughly half of the nation's domestic sewage and a fifth of its industrial wastewater.[19]

A master plan to improve the worsening environmental conditions in the basin has just been drafted. Korea is paying $4.1 million just for preparation of the plan—a measure of the importance it attaches to the cleanup.

The plan maps a four-pronged approach: better management of hazardous solid wastes; pre-processing of coal for *ondol* heating briquettes to make them burn cleaner; pollution-control loans to spur investment in antipollution equipment, waste-recovery facilities, cleaner production techniques, and factory relocation; and an industrial air-pollution control program for Incheon.

The Nanjido dump? The smelly eyesore would be converted into a sanitary landfill in which the excavated area would be small, rubbish promptly covered, and scavenging banned.

Eventually, the site may become part of a vast park that planners hope one day will grace the banks of a revitalized Han River.

* * *

But environmental decay in Asia is not confined to densely-settled, industrialized areas.

Take a look, for example, at one of the most remote and undeveloped parts of Thailand: its southern extremity.

To call this part of Thailand the "deep south" may be an understatement.

It's so deep that it sometimes seems to have only the most tenuous connection with the rest of the country.

A glance at the map helps explain its distinctiveness.

Geographically, Thailand resembles the head of an elephant—the animal that adorned the national flag when the country was known as Siam, and is still something of a national symbol.

The "trunk" is a thin isthmus, barely 40 miles wide in places, dangling down to the Malay peninsula. Thailand's southern region lies at the tip of the elephant's trunk.

Much of the area is closer to the Malaysian capital of Kuala Lumpur, to Singapore, or to the Indonesian city of Medan than to the Thai capital of Bangkok.

Culturally, the south has a special identity.

Calling themselves *Thai pak tai*—southern Thais—the people of the region tend to dress, speak, and worship differently than the rest of their countrymen.

The white skullcaps and waist sashes worn by many men, and the head scarves and long batik skirts and blouses on women, are a sartorial legacy of centuries of rule under a Malay empire and the subsequent local fiefdoms of Malay rajahs.

Malay words punctuate the southern Thai dialect.

The squat, onion-shaped domes of mosques testify to the predominance of Islam in these southernmost reaches of the world's largest Buddhist country.

Economically, the region is unevenly endowed.

It's rich in two of Thailand's leading export commodities—producing 95 per cent of its exports of rubber and 85 per cent of its tin. The country is the world's third-ranking supplier of both.

But geographical isolation has hindered development. The area was linked to the rest of the country by a road passable in all weather, for example, only in the 1960s.

And it still lacks deep-water port facilities for shipping out its bales of rubber and ingots of tin.

The south is just beginning to emerge from a traditional agrarian existence centered on fish, rice, and coconuts. Ninety per cent of southern Thais live in rural areas, subsisting on a household income averaging only a few hundred dollars a year.

Perhaps the most distinguishing natural feature of southern Thailand is sprawling Songkhla Lake.

Larger in area than the Dead Sea (395 square miles) and longer than Lake Constance (62 miles), the lake ranks as the biggest in Thailand and one of the biggest in Asia.

Part freshwater lake and part inland sea, it is actually a system of lagoons connected to the Gulf of Thailand.

Songkhla Lake and its surrounding basin support a population of 1 million people who depend on its waters for fishing, crop irrigation, industry, and commerce. But this vital resource is coming under increasing strain.

The competing demands for its water are threatening the delicate balance among the fresh, brackish, and salt waters that mingle along its length.

The pressures of nascent urbanization, too, are starting to be felt.

The two cities that anchor its southern end, Haadyai and Songkhla, with a combined population of about 200,000, are growing at a rate of more than 4 per cent a year—much of it from immigration.[20]

Songkhla has occupied the shores of the lake that bears its name for over 1,000 years of richly-textured history as a pirate stronghold, Chinese enclave, and outpost of the Srivijaya empire which ruled this part of Southeast Asia from the 7th to 13th centuries.

Long rows of weather-stained wooden shophouses, lining one of the narrow downtown streets, back up directly on the lake. Behind them, Thailand's largest fishing port—a confusion of bobbing boats, bawling vendors, nose-assaulting smells, and baskets slithering with the day's catch— stretches more than four miles along the lakefront.

Haadyai, its younger and more trendy sister city 16 miles away, is a booming shopping mecca for bargain-priced consumer goods smuggled from Singapore and Malaysia.

The fast pace of the city's modernization has not, regrettably, included sewage disposal. It is dumped into a *klong* or canal that empties, five miles downstream, into Songkhla Lake.

Industrialization is a relative newcomer, but already 15 large factories have sprung up on the main road between the two cities.

While Songkhla Lake is starting to show signs of stress, it is still no cesspool. Only a few years ago, it probably would have been allowed to degenerate into an environmental disaster, unnoticed until too late.

Not, fortunately, today. The Thai government has manifested enough concern to hire foreign experts to draw up a master plan to safeguard the lake ecosystem.

A multinational team of engineers, hydrologists, ecologists, and others is now at work on the campus of Prince of Songkhla University. The resulting plan is expected to, among other things, lead to upgrading the water-supply systems of the two cities and erecting a "salinity barrier" across the lake to separate fresh water from salt water.

To finance the undertaking, the government took the unparalleled step of borrowing $3 million—the first time it ever had done so for purely planning purposes of any kind.

Such a commitment, in a far-from-wealthy developing country such as Thailand, offers unmistakable monetary proof of rising environmental awareness.

## JANAKPUR, NEPAL

This forlorn little Indian-border town boasts a local official called a Conservator of Forests—but precious few forests left to conserve.

The Conservator is a balding forester whose principal contact with forest products these days is the reams of papers brought to his desk for signing by sarong-clad subordinates.

Like a shore-duty admiral or a hangar-bound pilot, the forester-turned-bureaucrat seems caged in his airless office.

The walls behind his husky shoulders are hung with faded black-and-white photographs showing the Conservator in sylvan settings presumably long since leveled. His deskwork is punctuated by wistful gazes out the window, and his conversation by long silences.

Perspiring over a glass of hot, milky tea in the drippy heat, he can well remember that as recently as 1950 this area was thickly wooded.

Today as he surveys his domain, he sees almost nothing but treeless flatlands of tiny rice plots and straw-roofed mud huts.

The naked plain sweeps all the way from the foothills of the Himalayas, rising blue in the haze on the northern horizon, into India about 12 miles south of here.

Deprived of moisture-retaining forest cover, the rivers that spill from the mountains across the plain are now dry beds of sun-bleached gravel much of the year. In the rainy season, waters gathered in the Himalayas pour unimpeded into India, bringing devastating floods to its northern states.

So acute is the shortage of firewood—in an area that a generation ago had virtually nothing else to offer but wood—that when the government recently distributed firewood at 9 rupees per cartload (70 cents, or about a day's wages), people flocked from 15 miles away. By bullock-drawn cart, that's a round-trip journey of two to three days.

This environmental and human tragedy is the ironic result of a justly-celebrated "advance" which turned out to be disastrous for the forests.

Malaria-carrying mosquitoes had kept this mountain kingdom's sunken southern frontier, known as the Terai, virtually uninhabited. Once the malaria was eradicated, settlers swarmed in from Nepal's hills and India—axes in hand.

The virgin soil beneath the trees was agriculturally rich, and the Terai was speedily cleared for farms, most of it occurring in the past 20 years. Today only 5 per cent of the region remains forested.

* * *

The stripping of Nepal's Terai is sadly symptomatic of what is befalling forests throughout the world.

Since just 1950, according to the United Nations' Food and Agriculture Organization (FAO), the earth has lost one-half of its forests.[1] Asia, which contains some of the world's largest and most productive tropical forests, is being shorn of its trees at the rate of 12,000 acres a day—an area half the size of Switzerland cut every year.[2]

At that pace, Malaysia may be denuded in 12 years, the Philippines in 14 years, and Thailand in 21 years.[3] Long leading wood exporters, all three countries now import logs or are about to do so.

The villain in this arboreal carnage has traditionally been the commercial loggers. They have certainly chopped their share of Asia's forests. But new, more scientific studies of the problem point the finger at a less likely culprit: the indigenous residents themselves.[4]

As many as 80 million Asians—more than the entire population of North Africa—make their livelihood from shifting cultivation. Known by various terms across the continent (such as *chena, jhum, kaingin,* or *podu*) and in English often as "slash-and-burn" agriculture, the practice involves clearing a patch of forest land, working it for two or three years, and then moving on.

This system of hack-as-you-go farming may have worked well enough when the forests were larger and the nomadic farmers fewer. But today the forests are being felled for random fields at a much faster rate than they can replenish themselves.

A recent survey of Asia's forest resources by the FAO reports that farmers practicing shifting cultivation now destroy more forest acreage than do logging companies. Forests are disappearing most rapidly, it finds, in areas where population is most dense and shifting cultivation most prevalent.

It's not simply that these farm families cannot, so to speak, see the woods for the trees—cannot see the lasting damage to the forest environment wreaked by their removal of a swatch of trees. The perpetrators are also prime victims. They suffer directly from shrinking forest habitat, declining soil fertility, and increasing erosion. But shifting cultivation, practiced by their kinsmen for centuries, is for most of them the only way of life they know.

The other main indigenous demand on Asia's forests is for firewood.

To most Westerners, firewood is purely recreational—a few sticks for a cosy campfire during a tenting vacation, or logs for a cheery glow in a living-room fireplace. But nearly half of humanity, including most Asians, rely on firewood every day to cook their food. And for many, it is also their only source of warmth on cold days and nights.

Almost half of all the wood cut each year in the world is estimated to be used as fuel, over four-fifths of it by the poor in developing nations.[5] In China, for example, at least three times more wood is burned as fuel in rural areas than is produced as timber.[6]

Despite so heavy a harvest of firewood, it falls increasingly short of meeting the need. Some 1.1 billion people—nearly one out of every four inhabitants of the earth—are reckoned by the FAO to have experienced a wood fuel shortage in 1980. Eighty per cent of them are Asians.[7]

In India, nearly half of whose energy consumption comes from firewood and from forest and farmyard wastes, firewood is now rationed in certain regions.[8]

Commercial logging, meanwhile, is a long way from ceasing to be a problem. Exporting logs and forest products offers a tempting source of foreign exchange. Logs have earned three of the largest exporters (Indonesia, Malaysia, and the Philippines) a combined total of $2.3 billion a year.[9] Few poor Asian countries can resist such ready cash.

Efforts to curtail logging run up against two other hinderances. One is that the traditional role of the government forest departments in many Asian countries is to earn revenue by exploiting the forests, rather than to protect them. The other is endemic governmental corruption which permits considerable illegal logging.

On the forest-rich island of Mindanao in the southern Philippines, drivers of trucks laden with logs can be seen openly handing peso banknotes to the military guards at checkpoints set up to prevent just such illegal plunder.

Even where commercial logging is controlled, it often inadvertently seals the doom of forest lands. The trails blazed into the forests by loggers frequently serve as the entryways for settlers who stream in to establish permanent colonies.[10]

Replanting hasn't yet taken root. Worldwide, only 1 acre of tropical forest is planted for every 13 acres felled. In Asia, a mere 5 per cent of the land cleared is being reforested.[11]

All, however, is not gloom. The destruction has reached such alarming proportions that it has become difficult to ignore. Some signs of hope:

- Deforestation has come to be recognized as a serious problem, for the first time, by governments throughout the nonindustrialized world where most of the forests lie.
- Many of these countries are now taking steps to conserve their dwindling reserves. Major timber-growing nations, including Indonesia, Malaysia, and the Philippines, which together supply over 80 per cent of the world's tropical hardwood exports, have clamped limits on logging and log exports.*
- Replenishing what has been lost is gaining higher priority. The first sizeable reforestation programs are being introduced in many countries. Malaysia, for one, plans to re-seed over 1 million acres. Money currently spent on tree-planting will be doubled by the $182 million worth of projects now on the drawing-boards.[12]

And trees, after all, do grow faster in the tropics than any other place on the planet.

\* \* \*

The change is etched sharply here in Nepal.

The remnants of the Terai forests, which so recently were allowed (and even encouraged) to be leveled, are now patrolled by armed government guards to ward off firewood poachers.

And a few tracts are being returned to forest.

Four-hundred nurseries have been set up, growing 9 million seedlings. Land is being reforested at an average pace of 6,000 acres per year. This is still only one-twentieth of the rate at which the World Bank calculates Nepal must plant trees to meet future fuelwood demands alone.[13] But it is a start.

---

* Indonesia began a phase-out in 1980; the Philippines has restricted log exports since 1974 and plans to phase it out altogether; Malaysia has been reducing log export quotas for several years.

One such beginning is being made west of here near the village of Sagarnath. Some 25,000 acres are being replanted with fast-growing trees that can start to be harvested for firewood and other uses within 10 years, while being continually renewed to maintain a forest cover.

Besides restoring a bit of forest to the Terai, the government project is trying to demonstrate that forests and rural villagers — rather than one having to give way to the other — can profitably coexist.

The plantations of Eucalyptus, teak, a local tree called *Sissoo*, and other fast-maturing varieties will provide villagers an important new source of firewood. Wood makes up 85 per cent of the domestic fuel consumed in Nepal.

In the present shortage, firewood is being shipped in from as far as 100 miles away. It is sold at a government depot for 25 rupees (about $2) for a *quintal*, or roughly one week's supply of cooking fuel for an average-sized family.

Since the cost may amount to several days' wages, many villagers instead are burning dried cow dung mixed with straw, thereby robbing their cropland of manure fertilizer.

Developing fuelwood plantations such as these has come to be known as "social forestry" — a concept that has not, however, always met universal social acceptance.

While many of the projects attract enthusiastic local support, others draw criticism. Critics charge that plantations of a few fast-growing species of trees are environmentally inferior to natural, variegated forests and detrimental to soil fertility. They claim that the firewood often is shipped off to cities and industries, bypassing villagers.

Local protests have occasionally erupted, as when farmers in southern India uprooted 10 million Eucalyptus seedlings in a government nursery.[14]

Even reforestation, it seems, is neither simple nor noncontroversial.

The plantations near here, however, give all appearances of being among the more popular. While growing a future supply of firewood, they are providing jobs and land to local people who previously had neither.

The two-year-old plantations now employ 300 laborers in an area of high rural unemployment, and eventually expect to hire 850 full-time and 800 others part-time during the monsoon season.

A smaller number of landless families are receiving land to farm. They're part of an experiment in a system known as *Taungya* — pioneered successfully in other parts of Asia and Africa — in which agricultural crops are raised along with the forests.

One of the recipients is a 27-year-old Nepali, slight of build and broad of smile, named Som Bahadur Thokar Lama. Unhappy as a mechanic's assistant in the hills, he moved two years ago (with his wife, toddler daughter, and assorted relatives) into a mud house in a village on the plantation.

He spends part of each day working on the forestry project and the rest tending his allotment of corn growing between the rows of newly-planted trees. Under his care, the land performs double-duty during the young trees' first two years, and the trees benefit from more intensive weeding.

Hill-bred Mr. Lama complains good-naturedly about the hardships here in the Terai, but says they're worth it just to have land to work.

"I came to this jungle, with its mosquitoes and its farms inside of forests," he says through an interpreter, "because I got my own land."

The project was intended to be copied elsewhere in Nepal—and it already is. Similar reforestation of another 25,000 acres of cut-over lands is being planned in the Kathmandu and Pokhara valleys. A series of such projects is being studied, meanwhile, for other parts of the Terai.

One day, perhaps, Nepal's Conservators of Forests may have something more to conserve than their woodsy memories.

# Physical and Intellectual
# Not-So-Well-Being

ANGORAM, PAPUA NEW GUINEA

We all think we know what the South Pacific must be like.

A vivid image has been etched for us in art, literature, and music—the impressionistic masterpieces that Tahiti evoked from Gauguin . . . the adventure stories of Robert Louis Stevenson, the last of them penned in his beloved Samoa . . . the lyrical strains of Rodgers and Hammerstein's *South Pacific*.

The image has been reinforced by countless Hollywood "South Sea island" films, and by every poster of Oceania that ever adorned a travel agent's office.

This is the South Pacific of blue lagoons, swaying palms, and cascades of bougainvillea. It is a vision of islanders living in carefree splendor, sarongs round their waists and frangipani blossoms in their hair.

The place has been indelibly stamped as a tropical paradise—a notion that the local tourist industry has done nothing to dispel.

Like most such reputations, it is part reality and part fantasy.

The stunning "Bali Ha'i" scenery is real enough. But if, back in the mists of time, life on the islands might ever have been as idyllic as the setting, today it's no Eden.

Despite a cornucopia of indigenous food—tropical fruits, green vegetables, root crops, wild game on larger islands, fish and shellfish almost everywhere—the diets of Pacific islanders are deteriorating. Malnutrition is a growing menace.

Although there is no known shortage of local staple food anywhere in the South Pacific, enormous quantities of food are imported.

The reasons why islanders are eating differently than their forebears range from complex changes in the societies to simple changes in tastes.

But the cost is heavy, both financially and nutritionally.

Papua New Guinea, the region's largest country, for example, spends nearly as much money to import food as petroleum.[1]

Along with it, the country has unwittingly imported problems. Many of the new foods are nutritionally inferior to the traditional ones they replace.

Government health officials estimate that Papua New Guineans get only 80 per cent of the food energy they need. They rate malnutrition as a major cause of infant and child deaths, and of stunted learning ability among children.[2]

None of the food newcomers is more pervasive—or more ironic—than imported canned fish.

Although surrounded by vast seafood resources and a net exporter of fish to other parts of the world, the South Pacific region supplies less than half of its own domestic demand. All the island countries import canned fish, mostly mackerel from Japan.[3]

Its popularity makes it one of the fastest-moving items in trading stores. To islanders unencumbered by its less-visible disadvantages, canned fish is a godsend—easier than fresh or dried fish to transport, store, serve, and often cheaper as well.

Efforts are now being made, however, to stem this canned-fish tide. And they are succeeding, in a small way, here in Papua New Guinea.

One of the last places on earth to be explored by Europeans, the country— occupying the eastern part of the island of New Guinea—took quickly to this type of Western convenience food. Canned fish swiftly became 70 per cent of all fish consumed,[4] but now may be beginning to ebb.

The battle for the palates of Papua New Guineans starts here in the north of the country.

This region is dominated by the broad, twisting presence of the Sepik River—one of the world's great rivers as measured by the volume of water carried. The name itself, aptly, means "big river."

Wide as a lake and dark as chocolate as it sweeps past this old German colonial station, the Sepik looks like a most unpromising source of fish. But its waters here run as deep as 150 feet, and teem with aquatic life.

The river has long supplied fish for villagers' own consumption. It also yields crocodiles (*pukpuk*, in the Pidgin English spoken here). In surrendering their skins for high-fashion shoes and handbags, they provide many local people the only cash they ever see. A five-footer fetches 70 kina, or about $75.

But as a national food larder, the Sepik remained almost untapped—until now.

In what may be their first contact with organized government, the village fishermen have been singled out for help by their government in Port Moresby. They are supplied (at or near cost) the basic fishing gear that most of them lack, such as gill-nets, buckets, and knives.

Better equipped, the fishermen are hauling bigger catches into their dug-out canoes. They dry-salt the surplus and sell it to a newly-built fishery.

The fish—*tilapia*, known locally as *solpis*—emerges in plastic packets containing half a pound of fillets, enough to feed six people.

Shipped to other parts of the country, the product is a resounding success. "We easily sell all we can produce," says a fishery supervisor. That has amounted so far to a modest output of little more than 20 tons a year.

So prized are the fish, however, that they are changing eating habits. Priced at half a kina (about 43 cents), a packet is cheaper than imported canned fish—and converting canned-fish eaters by the hundreds.

* * *

In nutrition and health, few Asians are any better off than Papua New Guineans. And many are far worse.

A resident of the 26 developing countries for which figures are available can expect to live to an average age of 57.5 years. That's 15 years less than the average American or Western European.

Life expectancy in India is just 52 years. In Nepal, it's 48, and in Bangladesh, a tragically youthful 46.[5]

Medical care is usually elusive, and often nonexistent. A physician, in those 26 Asian developing countries, serves an average of 7,500 persons.[6] Since most doctors work in cities, the scarcity is much greater in rural areas. In the United States, by contrast, the ratio is one physician per 580 persons.

At the bottom of the health-care league are impoverished nations such as Nepal, where there is a physician for every 25,000 people. Specialists are even rarer. The country has a pediatrician for every 209,000 children.[7]

What these statistics mean in practical terms, according to the World Health Organization (WHO) of the United Nations, is that over two-thirds of the people in developing Asia lack regular access to a trained health worker.[8]

A major, if not overriding, reason is that these poor lands simply cannot afford to provide better health services.

Governments in low-income Asia spend $5 or less per person a year on health. Bangladesh, one of the poorest, spends a mere 75 cents per head. West Germany, meanwhile, invests a corresponding $700 per person.[9]

Yet those developing countries that are least served are precisely those in greatest need.

Their populaces, like that of Papua New Guinea, are often undernourished. Residents of the 14 major Asian developing countries for which the World Bank has figures consume an average of less than the bare minimum of daily calories that the body is reckoned to require.[10]

In a region where many of the most widespread illnesses are transmitted by water, less than a third of the population (as we have seen) has access to safe water.[11]

And developing Asia is plagued by dread diseases that have been spared (or long eradicated from) more-fortunate parts of the globe, such as leprosy and malaria. It is infested with ailments associated with poverty, such as diarrhea, lice, and worms.

As if these weren't hazards enough, the very atmosphere inside the humble hut of many an Asian peasant has been found to be among the most polluted on earth.

A WHO study in India discovered homes with open fires to have 10 times the air contamination of some of Europe's more industrialized cities. The rural women laboring over such fumy, wood fires were rated only slightly better off than coke-oven workers.[12]

\* \* \*

Just as it is hard to imagine the inhabitants of the dreamy South Pacific isles spooning their fish from cans, so it takes some effort to picture them as wracked by ill health.

But the stereotype of the robust Pacific islander, frolicking through an outdoor life of bucolic healthfulness, also needs revising.

The truth is that the South Pacific, alas, isn't a particularly healthy place in which to live.

A newborn baby faces a much more chancy prospect of surviving here than in the Western industrialized world. The infant mortality rate, as low as 14 per 1,000 live births in a country like the United States, soars to 87 in Kiribati (formerly the Gilbert Islands) and 105 in Papua New Guinea.[13]

The survivors can expect a foreshortened life span. Residents of Kiribati, Papua New Guinea, and the Solomon Islands, for instance, live an average of less than 54 years.[14]

Such cruel statistics are an eloquent plea for improved health care. But for poor, isolated island societies, the usual prescription—more doctors and expensive facilities—is clearly the wrong remedy.

Tonga, one of the smallest and least endowed Pacific countries—a string of islands 5,000 watery miles southeast of Papua New Guinea—spends only one-tenth as much money on health care as does wealthy Japan.* Yet it is managing to raise its standard of health using a basic, community-level approach.

One who appreciates the improvement is a young mother of three named Sarah Manisela.

Her village, known as Houma, a cluster of weathered wooden houses and huts roofed with brown coconut fronds, never had medical facilities. Whenever her first two children needed medical attention, she had to transport them across the island to the capital Nuku'alofa—a 10-mile trip that involved either three bus rides or a plodding trek by horse-drawn cart.

Caring for her third child has become much simpler. Today she has brought the baby to a little health center right in the village. Here the child is routinely checked every month. She says the baby is healthier, and so is the rest of her family.

The health center is a small, cement-block building, as gleamingly white as a freshly-starched nurse's uniform. The waiting room is nearly filled by a dozen or so village women, most of them with children.

Mrs. Manisela's baby is being examined by health officer Ofa Teu, a bull-necked young man with sympathetic eyes that soften the heavy features of his face. A stethoscope dangles over his white cloak.

Mr. Teu is what is sometimes romantically referred to as a "barefoot doctor," trained locally in basic medical care by the WHO, and then dispatched into the doctorless countryside.

He has run this center since it opened two years ago, spending mornings here and in the afternoons making home visits. Assisted by a nurse, he sees an average of more than 20 patients a day at the clinic—40 to 50 on Mondays.

Two days a week, he conducts "baby clinics" for mothers in surrounding villages. He also holds training sessions for women on caring for diarrhea and acute illness; makes home-sanitation inspections; and visits primary schools.

Since coming here, Mr. Teu says he has observed a marked improvement in the health of the 4,000 villagers whom the center serves. Long-term illness has decreased as ailments are treated more promptly. Diarrhea, once common, has become rare as sanitation conditions improve.

---

* $11 per capita, compared with $107 per capita by Japan (according to the World Health Organization, as reported by the Asian Development Bank, *Appraisal Report, Multi-Project Loan [Tonga]*, December 1979).

The health center, one of four in Tonga financed by foreign assistance, also is helping lighten the load on the hospital in the capital. While the number of Tongans receiving medical consultations has doubled with the coming of the health centers, the number of hospital patients has dropped by several thousand each year.

Perhaps the South Pacific can, one day, become a little more of a "paradise."

## MANILA, PHILIPPINES

Virginia lacks a high school education, but speaks three languages.

A linguist? No, she's a housemaid.

Virginia is trilingual simply because she has to be.

She speaks Ilocano because it's the native tongue of her home province (Benguet) in northern Luzon. She speaks Tagalog because it's the language of Manila where she works. And she uses English to communicate with her employers, most of whom have been Americans.

Technically speaking, a fourth language should be included in Virginia's linguistic repertoire: Pilipino, the hybrid national language.

Because the Philippines had no common tongue—over 70 languages and dialects are spoken, nine of them widely prevalent[1]—it was decided during the 1930s to concoct one. Based largely on Tagalog, it is understood by most anyone who, like Virginia, knows that language, although it remains little used.

In this national Tower of Babel, Virginia's polylingualism is far from exceptional. Virtually any Filipino who attends school, or marries someone from another province, or moves to another part of the country, or goes into business or government service, is compelled to learn another language.

Nor is the Philippines much different, in its language diversity, from much of the rest of developing Asia.

In the West, citizens of a country tend to share a common language. Indeed, the whole of Latin America (except Brazil) is linguistically united by Spanish. The few Western exceptions to the rule of one-country, one-language, such as Belgium, Switzerland, or Canada, are regarded as cultural oddities.

Consider, then, the cacophony of languages clattering across Asia:

## INDIA

"I cry," Jawaharlal Nehru, India's first prime minister, once lamented, "when I think that I cannot speak my own mother tongue as well as I can speak the English language."[2]

Fired by such nationalistic sentiments, the newly-independent India enshrined in its constitution the scrapping of the colonial language, as the official language, for a native tongue.

Out of the 1,652 languages spoken in the world's second most populous country, the founding fathers chose the one most widely used: Hindi. They proclaimed that in 15 years—in 1965—Hindi would erase the last traces of English as the language in which India communicates.[3]

It was a goal that was easier said—in whatever language—than done. More than 20 years after the transition deadline, and over 40 years after independence, India's official language remains a minority tongue.

While still the country's most widely spoken, Hindi is the first language of little more than a quarter of the population (28 per cent).[4] Recognizing this, a second tier of 14 languages has been designated as "national" languages.

Altogether, no fewer than 32 tongues are spoken by at least 100,000 people, according to the latest language census figures. These are led by Telugu and Bengali, each spoken by over 50 million people—more than speak many Western national languages, such as any of the Scandinavian or Slavic tongues.[5]

The other language groups in India stoutly resist efforts to extend the use of Hindi. The selection of the official language back in 1950, in fact, was acrimoniously debated and adopted in the constitutional body by a margin of one vote.[6]

More recently, opposition to the spread of Hindi produced riots in 1982 in the southern state of Karnataka, and formation of a Telugu political party which in 1983 gained control of the state of Andhra Pradesh.

So India remains a rich but confusing linguistic potpourri. Its very national anthem (*Jana Gana Mana*), sung daily by every Indian schoolchild, is written not in the official national language but in Bengali.[7]

The government-controlled All India Radio broadcasts nationally in 19 languages, including English. Its regional stations transmit in an additional 60 languages and dialects.[8]

The country's newspapers publish in a bewildering 84 languages—10 of them each used by 30 or more individual dailies and circulated among half a million or more readers.[9]

The English-language papers, fourth largest in number (105 dailies) and second largest in circulation (9.7 million), are elevated to an elite position by a readership that transcends regional language boundaries. They call themselves the "national press" and condescendingly refer to their Indian-language rivals as the "language press."[10]

The tainted, old colonial language of English which Hindi was supposed to supplant, ironically, may today be the nearest thing in India to a truly national language. It's the language of college instruction, of the courts, and—by an act of parliament—of the government itself.[11]

## PAKISTAN

Television viewers in Pakistan may not be offered much of a choice of channels—there is only one—but they may watch the news in any of three languages.

In Karachi, the news is aired at 5:40 p.m. in Urdu, the national language. This is followed 15 minutes later by the news in Sindhi, the provincial language. Then at 7:30 p.m. comes the news in English, a lively linguistic relic of the British Empire.[12]

As in the case of their large neighbor on the east, the presence of an anointed national language doesn't inhibit Pakistanis from communicating in a chorus of tongues, many mutually unintelligible.

Of the country's 1,156 newspapers, magazines, and other periodicals, one-third are published in languages other than Urdu—English and assorted regional languages.

Take, for instance, the province of Sind. On the newsstands of the nation's most populous province can be found 16 local daily newspapers in Urdu, 12 in Sindhi, 7 in English, and 3 in Gujerati.[13]

In gaining dominance as Pakistan's national language, Urdu has been handicapped by being something of a linguistic stepchild. Less than 300 years old as a full-fledged language—probably the youngest of the world's major tongues—it essentially consists of Hindi written in Arabic script.

It is a language originally spoken by only 7 per cent of the population, since most Urdu-speaking areas remained behind when Pakistan was partitioned from India in 1947.[14] Among those who knew no Urdu was the new nation's founder, Mohammed Ali Jinnah.[15]

Urdu is still striving for full recognition.

It only recently became the language of command in the Pakistan army.[16] Education in scientific fields continues to be conducted in English. Private schools, taught in English, are proliferating—180 of them established in the past six years in Lahore alone.[17] And programs in English occupy a fifth of the country's television broadcasting time.[18]

Even the national government itself doesn't really communicate in the national language. Chagrined, the National Language Authority is taking remedial measures. Training centers have been set up in federal ministries to teach government employees how to type and take shorthand in Urdu.[19]

## BANGLADESH

Language Day is a major national holiday in Bangladesh, celebrated every February with all the ritualistic fervor befitting the important role that language played in the violent birth of the country.

The language in this case is Bengali, spoken in this teeming quarter of the Indian subcontinent for millennia, under Moghul emperors, the British Raj while part of colonial India, and then the Pakistanis while designated as East Pakistan.

Although ranking among the world's most widely-spoken languages—the native tongue of far more people than either German, Italian, or French[20]— Bengali had always been linguistically subjugated.

A demand to make Bengali the official language of East Pakistan led to the fatal shooting by police in 1952 of four students—one of those explosive events that alters the course of a people's history. It sparked a nationalist campaign known as the Language Movement, a smoldering force in what erupted in 1971 into a bloody but successful war of independence.

Now commemorated annually as Language Day, the event draws hundreds of thousands of Bangladeshis—barefoot—to lay wreaths at a monument erected in Dhaka to the martyred students.

The annual observance also is the occasion for a rather more ironic ritual: an outpouring of statements bemoaning that Bengali (now often called Bangla) isn't more widely used in the country.

Despite the sacrifice of lives for the language, and the absence of other indigenous languages within the country (unlike India or Pakistan), Bangladesh's official tongue remains far from universal. And language is still an unsettled issue.

Schoolchildren in Bangladesh study, through their first 12 years, two compulsory languages—Bengali and English. At one time, they also had to learn Arabic, but this third required language was dropped in 1983.[21]

The more-exclusive private schools, where the country's high-achievers are educated, give strong emphasis to English.

So much of the government operates in English that the President, Gen. Hossain Mohammad Ershad, felt it necessary recently to order that all official proceedings be written in Bengali instead of English.[22]

Notwithstanding the Language Day rhetoric, English has its defenders.

Argues an editorial in *The Bangladesh Observer*—an influential Dhaka daily newspaper published, naturally, in English:

"English is part of our history. We have evolved with it and have been thinking in it for centuries. . . . We can neither ignore it, nor isolate it, without doing much injury to ourselves."[23]

## SRI LANKA

This island nation off the tip of India is only about the size of the American state of West Virginia, with fewer people than New York. But it has three authorized languages.

Sinhala, the tongue of the majority Sinhalese, is the country's "official" language. But Tamil, spoken by the Tamil minority, and English are designated as "national" languages in which·official business may be conducted.

Since the Sinhalese and Tamils, who form about 12 per cent of the population, are divided not only by language but frequently tense social relations, the English language is meant to perform something of a healing function.

The old colonial tongue is viewed as what President Junius Jayewardene called "a link language" between two communities often barely on speaking terms.[24]

## MALAYSIA

Nothing conveys the multilingualism of this country more graphically than the signboards, visible everywhere, on which Malay words in Roman letters coexist uneasily with Chinese ideograms and Indian script.

It was never supposed to be this way. The Malay language, now called Bahasa Malaysia, is assiduously cultivated as a device for unifying the diverse cultures that make up this nation of once-autonomous states and sultanates.

The language is gradually becoming the lone medium of instruction in public schools—replacing English in universities in 1983—while making steady inroads in the government and the professions.[25]

Yet, as the multilingual signboards·attest, the Malay-dominated government's promotion of Bahasa Malaysia meets resistance.

Many in the large minority of ethnic Chinese, and the smaller minority of ethnic Indians (mainly Tamils), find it irksome or even threatening. The two states comprising East Malaysia on the island of Borneo (Sabah and Sarawak) still use English as their official languages. And it took until 1981 for the first civil lawsuit to be tried in Malaysia in the country's national language.[26]

## SINGAPORE

The bustling city-state at the snout of the Malay peninsula would seem to face no problem of linguistic identity.

With its distinct character as a Chinese enclave in Southeast Asia—80 per cent Chinese in ethnic composition and consummately Confucian in organization and tone—Singapore would be presumed to be a stronghold of Chinese language.

Not so. Although assorted Chinese dialects (mainly Hokkien) are still spoken by most Singaporeans, English is fast becoming the country's first language.

A tongue that the British rulers were unable to impose on the colony they founded in 1819 is being adopted voluntarily today by independent Singapore.

The reasons here have less to do with linguistic diversity or national unification, however, than rapid modernization. Just as Singapore is obliterating its old cityscape of traditional Chinese shophouses for soaring skyscrapers, it is exchanging the tongue of its Chinese heritage for the language of international commerce and technology.

Prime Minister Lee Kuan Yew explains the growing primacy of English as "an inevitable consequence of our economic development."[27]

While the island nation continues to have four official languages—Chinese, Malay, Tamil, and English—the advance of English appears irreversible.

Fewer than 1 per cent of primary school pupils now enroll in schools where teaching is conducted in Chinese.[28] In 1987, English became the medium of instruction in all schools.

In a burst of ethnic zeal, Southeast Asia's only Chinese-language institution of higher learning was founded here in 1956. It was christened Nanyang University, meaning "South Seas" — a name symbolizing the wide horizons envisioned for it. In 1981, plagued by dwindling enrollment, the university was closed.[29]

This overwhelmingly Chinese nation now finds itself in the odd position of considering recruiting teachers and journalists from Hong Kong and Taiwan to keep the Chinese language alive.[30]

## VANUATU

The most extreme case of polylingualism in this polylingual region, however, may be the South Pacific country of Vanuatu.

The place has only 126,000 inhabitants, spread over some 80 scattered islands. But among them, they speak about 100 languages—distinct languages, that is, not dialects. This intense "language density" is reckoned to give Vanuatu more languages per capita than any other country in the world.[31]

There's a further linguistic complication. Administered jointly by Britain and France as the New Hebrides (or Nouvelles Hebrides) until its independence in 1980, Vanuatu has had to simultaneously absorb not one, but two Western colonial languages.

While both English and French remain official media of instruction in schools, Vanuatu is the only South Pacific country to designate in its constitution an indigenous tongue (the pidgin-like Bislama) as its national language.[32]

When the Fiji-based University of the South Pacific was seeking a site for its new Pacific languages institute, perhaps it was only natural that it chose Port Vila—the capital of this living language laboratory.

* * *

All this would have little more than passing cross-cultural interest were it not for evidence that a "language problem" may contribute to more fundamental problems.

It may impede the economic and social advancement of a developing country out of poverty and intellectual deprivation.

The indigenous languages of many Asian developing nations, for one thing, tend to be rather unsophisticated, linguistically speaking. Their vocabularies and grammatical structures frequently prove inadequate to convey the complicated terms and subtle shades of meaning required in modern communication.

In the Tagalog language spoken in the Philippines, for instance, the same adjective (*mainit*) means both "hot" and "warm," while another (*malamig*) is used to indicate both "cold" and "cool."

Gunnar Myrdal encountered the problem in his study of South Asia. In *Asian Drama*, he writes:

"The official indigenous languages are linguistically underdeveloped; complex concepts, especially in the technical and scientific fields, cannot be expressed in these languages."[33]

A large share of the printed word in Asia—both technical and literary—is published in non-Asian languages, particularly English. Intellectual matters tend to be conveyed in English in countries once ruled by the British and Americans: India, Malaysia, Pakistan, Philippines, Singapore, and Sri Lanka.

Two prime publishing centers in the region, Hong Kong and Singapore, issue nearly as many books in English as in the vernacular Chinese. Of the

3,041 titles published in the latest year for which figures are available (1978), 1,262 appeared in English and 1,534 in Chinese (plus 89 in Malay, 10 in Tamil, and a smattering in other languages).[34]

Aware of the inadequacy of many of the local tongues, scholars and language commissions are hard at work across the continent trying to linguistically enrich them.

In Bangladesh, the intellectual and scientific community has been enjoined by the government to compile lists of technical terms for incorporating into Bengali.[35]

In Malaysia, the Language and Culture Council (*Dewan Bahasa dan Pustaka*)—with help from a literate IBM computer—has larded the Malay language with more than 250,000 specialist terms coined for the various professions.[36]

These elites aren't the only ones, however, handicapped by Asia's language problems. The basic education of the masses also suffers.

In primary schools, pupils frequently are compelled to study two or more languages—not as foreign languages, but for everyday use. Many schoolchildren in India and Pakistan, for example, are taught several languages, each written in a different script.[37]

This heavy load of languages not only complicates pupils' learning of communication skills, but grossly overbalances their schooling with language study.

As educator Edmund J. King observes: "the curriculum of any child is bound to be congested on the linguistic side before anything else is learned."[38]

In secondary schools, the "congestion" is often compounded by requiring at least one Western language, such as English. "As in the primary schools," Mr. Myrdal notes, "language study crowds other subjects out of the curriculum and proficiency in languages becomes the yardstick of educational achievement."[39]

Amid such linguistic complexities, it may be small wonder that a stubbornly large proportion of Asians remains illiterate or semi-literate.

This continent—cradle of much of the world's earliest learning and home of some of its richest cultures—contains nearly three-quarters of mankind's illiterates, according to the United Nations.

They are estimated to total 387 million, or almost twice the population of the United States. And the number of Asians who can neither read nor write, although gradually declining in percentage terms, is increasing numerically because of population growth.[40]

In seven developing countries in the region, more than half of adults are illiterate. In India, the illiteracy rate is 64 per cent; in Bangladesh, 74 per cent; Pakistan, 76 per cent; and Nepal, 81 per cent.[41]

While many other factors are involved in illiteracy of such proportions, including inadequate educational facilities, the absence of a universal national language must play a part.

Even among the educated, the linguistic challenge leaves a substantial number of Asians semi-literate (or semi-illiterate). They acquire only a rudimentary grasp of any of their country's languages.

A recent survey by Hong Kong University, for instance, found many students to be proficient in neither Chinese nor English — destined for lives in a verbal and cultural no-man's-land.[42]

But perhaps the greatest detrimental impact of the "language problem" in developing Asia is simply that it diverts national resources and attention that might otherwise be devoted to these countries' urgent needs.

The division of countries into communal language groups . . . the campaigns for wider use of the national language . . . the efforts to enrich indigenous languages . . . the strain on educational systems struggling to teach multiple languages — however unavoidable these circumstances may be — are deadweights on the process of economic uplift.

# Harnessing Human Resources

Vic M. had all that most Filipinos might desire in life—a young family, a gleaming stainless-steel jeep, and a brisk little home fix-it business.

But he also had something else (also far from rare in these islands): a consuming determination to earn more money. And, in the end, it triumphed over the others.

One day Vic left behind his family, jeep, and fix-it customers—leaving in his wake air-conditioners and other appliances strewn in various stages of disrepair across Manila, without a word of explanation.

Puzzled customers who telephoned were informed that he had taken a job in Saudi Arabia.

*  *  *

Romy S. was secure but unhappy in the printing shop of one of the most desirable employers in Manila.

He'd rather repair electronic gadgets, and did as much of it as he could on the side.

So when the opportunity came, Romy chucked his printing career and went off to work at electronics in Saudi Arabia.

*  *  *

Tely S. was a church organist, relied on so totally by her little church in the bustling Malate district of Manila that there simply was no substitute organist.

Suddenly, without notice, she no longer turned up. The services slogged along without music for weeks before the church learned that Tely was working as a musician in Saudi Arabia.

* * *

Hundreds of young Filipinos like Vic, Romy, and Tely converge weekly on Manila International Airport.

The faintly bewildered looks . . . the teary farewells to jeepney-loads of relatives who have come to see them off . . . the stiff new jackets emblazoned with the names of construction companies in Riyadh or Dubai—have become familiar accompaniments to every flight departing to the Middle East.

It's all a well-worn routine, and the airport has adapted itself to cope with this new class of travelers. They are escorted through the check-in formalities and sped on their way almost before they realize it.

And when they return one day, laden with VCRs and "ghetto-blasters," they will use a separate passport lane reserved for overseas workers.

So it is at airports throughout developing Asia. Young laborers, who may never previously have ventured beyond their own villages, have become international jet-setters—pampered like visiting dignitaries.

And with good reason. In economic terms, they are VIPs.

For many countries in the region, they have become one of the most lucrative exports—in some cases, *the* most lucrative one.

Their home countries have come to rely on regularly shipping abroad some of their human capital. Not only does it help absorb surplus labor, but it earns hard, convertible currency—a scarce commodity in developing nations—to help buy products that must be imported and to repay foreign debts.

This overseas work force is the size of the population of many countries in the world. At any one time, some 4 million Asians are working temporarily abroad, mostly in the Middle East.

The influx of foreign workers into the Mideast since rising oil prices touched off an economic boom in the 1970s has made them more numerous than the indigenous workers in labor-importing Arab nations. Except for laborers from poorer Arab neighbor countries, Asians comprise the largest bloc.[1]

In the United Arab Emirates, foreigners make up 80 per cent of the population and 90 per cent of the work force, the majority of them Asians.[2]

Pakistan—a populous, labor-rich country which shares an Islamic heritage with the Persian Gulf nations—is the leading Asian manpower exporter.

With an estimated 2 million Pakistanis working in the Mideast, or roughly one out of every 10 persons of working age, the lure of employment abroad is

95

firmly rooted in the society. The phenomenon has entered the Urdu vernacular as *Dubai chalo* ("Let's go to Dubai").[3]

Another 1 million emigrant workers come from Pakistan's giant neighbor, India.[4]

Outside the Indian subcontinent, no Asian nation supplies more overseas workers than the Philippines. Some 650,000 Filipinos hold temporary jobs in other countries, nearly equalling the 700,000 new workers who enter the overcrowded domestic job market every year.

As with most Asian contract laborers abroad, the Filipinos are predominantly men. But women comprise 16 per cent, and their number, once negligible, is doubling every two years.[5]

Most of the Philippine workers are found in the Mideast, with a heavy concentration in one country: Saudi Arabia. The 250,000 or so Filipinos there amount to 5 per cent of the native population.[6]

Among other Asian sources of foreign labor, Thailand contributes over 350,000 workers,[7] Bangladesh and South Korea somewhat fewer,[8] Indonesia around 100,000,[9] and China about 40,000.[10]

For the labor-supplying countries, dispatching human resources across the globe is a billion-dollar-a-year enterprise that helps bolster often-fragile economies.

The wages sent back home by Asian overseas workers (often mandated by their governments) have mushroomed more than 30-fold since 1968, from $200 million to over $7 billion a year, according to a study by the International Labor Organization (ILO).

The remittances covered 75 per cent of Pakistan's trade deficit in 1982, nearly half of India's in 1980, and 22 per cent of Bangladesh's in 1982.[11]

The proceeds from Pakistan's army of emigrant workers over the past decade have done much to keep the country solvent—providing 53 per cent of the total foreign-exchange earnings and 10 per cent of the national income.[12]

In Thailand, the world's leading rice exporter, rice traditionally has been the top foreign-exchange earner. But it recently has been overtaken, first by tourism and now by remittances from Thai workers abroad (approaching $1 billion a year).[13]

In the Philippines, where overseas workers are required to send home from 50 to 70 per cent of their wages, remittances have eclipsed the earnings of the most-profitable export product, semiconductors.[14]

Despite the valuable contribution to the national economies, much of the money earned abroad is nonetheless squandered on consumer goods—often imported items that only worsen the trade deficits which the remittances are supposed to help alleviate.

The households of Pakistani emigrant workers, for example, were shown in a study to spend nearly two-thirds of their remittance income on increased consumption. Only 13 per cent went for "productive investment."[15]

Filipino workers, similarly, upon returning home (either to visit or remain) arrive loaded like Santa Clauses with an average of $1,050 worth of merchandise apiece.[16]

The export of labor is hardly an unalloyed blessing. While it does bring in hard currency and soak up excess manpower, it also creates personnel dislocations and skills shortages at home—in poor, developing countries that can ill afford these problems.

At the upper levels of the labor market, there is a steady siphoning away of skilled professionals vital to nation-building. Pakistan, for instance, loses half its medical graduates every year. About 30 per cent of India's engineers emigrate after finishing their training.[17]

Even if remittances offset the lost costs of their training, these talented elites are difficult to replace. In the Philippines, a recent study estimates that at present enrollment rates and no emigration, the country will need 16 years to produce the number of physicians it needs. But at the pace at which doctors are now leaving the country, it will take 26 years.[18]

Highly-trained professionals, however, fill only a fraction of the Asian jobs overseas. In the Mideast, they comprise little more than a few per cent. The great exodus occurs among those with lesser skills or virtually none, such as mechanics and construction workers. Their departure confronts the home country not so much with a "brain drain" as a "brawn drain."

Although still flooded with surplus labor, the countries frequently find shortages developing in certain fields. And job turnover rates become high— and costly.

At the giant Tarbela hydroelectric dam in northern Pakistan, engineers complain that control-room technicians leave for work in the Mideast as fast as they can train them. Similar frustrations are voiced at Manila Electric Company and oil refineries in the Philippines.[19]

The long-term upgrading of the qualifications of the national work force—and the individual worker—also may suffer. Landing a job overseas often means taking a step downward in skills in order to take a step upward in pay.

With the earnings of Filipinos employed abroad averaging twice as much as those of Manila office workers (according to a survey by the country's labor ministry), many settle for overseas jobs below their capabilities just to cash in.[20]

Female emigrant workers from the Philippines offer a prime example. Overseas employment officials say wealthy households in the Mideast are filled with Filipino housemaids who gave up low-paying careers as school-teachers back home. They can make two to three times as much money working as domestic servants.[21]

Maintaining a large work force overseas also sets off social reverberations.

There's the strain of family separation. Workers go off to toil in an alien society, normally on a two-year contract, leaving behind families dependent on the sometimes-erratic remittance checks of absent breadwinners. The distant separation seems to spawn endless suspicions over the amount of money being sent home and how it is being spent.

The conspicuous consumption of the newly-monied families of many over-seas workers has sometimes had an unsettling effect on the impoverished communities where they often live. In Thailand, the free-spending wives of foreign laborers are disparagingly (and perhaps a little enviously) called *khun-nai-Saudi*—"Saudi ladies."[22]

There are signs, however, suggesting that the overseas employment bonanza may have peaked. Doors in the host countries are beginning to swing closed a bit.

Harsher economic conditions are chilling the old welcome. Industrialized nations are beset by economic slowdown and rising unemployment. The Mideast is coping with an oil glut and switching to more capital-intensive and high-technology development projects.

Another pressure, having nothing to do with economics, is at work in the Mideast: growing concern that the local cultures may be "contaminated" by hordes of foreigners.

Asian workers are stamping their presence on the Gulf region. Theaters and video shops feature films from India. Newsstands sell publications in Hindi and Urdu. Hotels vibrate to the music of Filipino bands.

Asians also take the blame for more sinister influences. The increasing use of narcotics is traced to drugs from the Indian subcontinent. A lucrative trade has sprung up in forged documents for overseas workers.[23] A total of 2,000 Pakistanis were recently reported by their country's interior minister to be in jail for various crimes in Saudi Arabia.[24]

While the World Bank forecasts continued growth in the expatriate job market in the Mideast over the next decade,[25] most other observers expect a decline. The ILO reports that salary offers already have dropped by 15 to 20 per cent.[26]

Nearly all Gulf countries have recently tightened visa controls and stepped up job training among their own nationals.[27] Bahrain—where 40 per cent of the population of 350,000 are foreigners—now requires imported technicians to have Bahraini assistants, and is considering limiting the proportion of aliens working in commercial establishments to 10 per cent.[28]

At least two Gulf nations, Saudi Arabia and Kuwait, also now demand certificates of "good moral character" on each incoming overseas worker.[29]

In Western Europe, the countries hosting the largest numbers of immigrant laborers (chiefly Mediterraneans, but also many Asians)—Belgium, Britain, France, Switzerland, and West Germany—all are taking steps to reduce the influx.[30]

Even Singapore, a fast-industrializing Asian nation which employs thousands of workers from poorer neighboring countries, plans to send them all home. The government intends to phase out all 150,000 foreign workers—among a population of 2.5 million—by 1992. As a start, it has slapped a fee of 120 Singapore dollars (about $60) per month on each of the island-nation's 9,000 foreign housemaids, 7,000 of them from the Philippines.[31]

In the face of such resistance, the overseas employment indicators point omniously downward.

The number of Filipinos in Gulf countries is declining for the first time in a decade.[32] Remittances from Pakistanis working abroad are tapering off.[33] South Koreans employed in the Gulf region have decreased by one-fifth.[34]

If the trends continue, many Asian developing countries will face a stern new challenge. Not only will they lose an important outlet for their surplus labor, but they will have to absorb hundreds of thousands of workers returning—jobless—from overseas.

Pakistan alone, warns a recent study by the ILO, may be saddled with as many as 750,000 returning emigrant laborers by the end of the decade.[35]

The problems imposed by a drying up of the Mideast job well could quickly devalue those billions of petrodollars in remittances which Asian nations have so voraciously pumped from it.

## NEAR PESHAWAR, PAKISTAN

The last rays of autumn sun glint across some of the last stretches of level terrain to be found in Pakistan before it trails off into the Hindu Kush mountains to the northwest.

Last season's leaves are fluttering with golden flourishes to the earth, where next season's crop of winter wheat is already poking tender green sprouts expectantly into the brisk air.

The byways are alive with villagers, threading single-file along footpaths rimming their fields or striding dirt roads to the nearest market town.

Nearly all are men. A chance encounter between male villagers, either along the way or in the village, is no mere passing-nod-and-smile occasion. The two men stop, grasp both of each others' hands, and bow, the face beneath their turban or skullcap fixed in an expression of the most solemn concern.

Crossing paths with a village woman could hardly be less ceremonious. The few women seen out and about draw up their robes to cover all but their eyes. When a group of men and a group of women approach each other along a country path, the women step aside and turn their backs on the passing men.

Back home in the villages, women tread an equally restricted path in life.

In their own houses, one of the principal rooms is normally off-limits to them. This is a room, found in the typical baked-mud houses in this part of Pakistan, furnished with heavy wooden cots strung with rope webbing (known as *charpoys*), its walls hung with photographs, framed newspaper clippings, and other family mementos.

The room is set aside for the men of the house to host other village men or visitors — to discuss village business, or just to chat and gossip.

A visitor calling at one of these homes might easily gain the impression, indeed, that no women reside there. They are nowhere to be seen.

The reality, however, is that not only could village households scarcely function without women, but that the house entertaining the visitor probably is full of women at the time. They are only shunted discreetly out of sight.

For the ancient Islamic practice of *purdah* — the Urdu word for "curtain" has lent its name to the custom of hiding women from the presence of men and strangers — is still rigorously observed here in the countryside.

In Pakistan's metropolis, Karachi, far to the south on the Arabian Sea, women are freer of such strictures. They can be seen working in offices, dining in restaurants and traveling in airplanes with their husbands. They even turn up on television — reading the news in English or, in a touch of irony, advertising the Muslim Commercial Bank.

But three-quarters of Pakistani women live in rural areas, where their role, as with those near Peshawar, is far more circumscribed.

* * *

In their repression, they have plenty of company throughout Asia. Women just may comprise the continent's largest single underdeveloped resource.

Asian women, by and large, are consigned to the domestic world of home and family by economic, cultural, and religious constraints more enduring than any that have prevailed in the West.

Whatever the personal toll of frustrated individuality and dashed yearnings — and it must be considerable — half of the population is denied full participation in a developing society which needs to marshal all the talent it can.

Most women in this region live the sort of existence that would be a nightmarish anathema to Betty Friedan. The focus — indeed, frequently the perimeter — is to serve one's husband and other elders, bear and rear children, and perform household tasks.

Since these responsibilities are rarely either paid or valued in financial terms, women are regarded as dependent on the men who earn money outside the home, with all the inferior status which such dependency confers.

While a son is counted an asset, a daughter is a liability.

As a future breadwinner and investment for old age (in societies where pensions and Social Security are generally unknown), a male child receives most of a family's care and whatever it can afford for such refinements as education.

A daughter, however, is viewed as a transitory member of the family, to be brought up as sparingly as possible and married off at the earliest opportunity.

In an acutely underdeveloped country like Bangladesh, more than 70 per cent of women are married before reaching the age of 20. The legal age of marriage there has been raised only in recent years progressively from 14 to 16 and now to 18. But few marriages are registered, and in rural villages are found married girls as young as 9. (The latest national census reports 7 per cent of girls aged 10 to 14 as married.)[1]

In neighboring India, over half (56 per cent) of women are wed before leaving their teenage years.[2] In Indonesia, the region's third most populous country, girls may legally marry at 16 and in rural areas many do so earlier.[3]

"Women," as a Chinese proverb avers, "hold up half the sky." But the hard fact that they uphold virtually all Asian households passes largely unheralded.

Besides raising a family (usually large), a wife is the prime provider of the family's shelter, food, water, clothing, and fuel — without the aid of supermarkets, kitchen appliances, sewing machines, or often even electricity and running water.

In rural areas, where most Asian women live, she is also the chief farm-hand. Household chores must be interspersed with agricultural tasks such as drying, husking, and winnowing grain, as well as looking after the bullock, goats, chickens, or other family livestock.

Most crops harvested in Asia are processed, and most livestock cared for, by women.

It adds up to a working day for rural wives often 12 to 18 hours long—spent almost entirely stooping, bending, or squatting.

Here's the daily routine of a typical rural Bangladesh housewife, as chronicled by a woman journalist in that country:[4]

A village woman's day begins at 5 a.m. She wakes up and washes the dishes and pots. Usually ashes are used for washing, which is done in a nearby pond. Then she cleans the house, releases the poultry, and collects eggs.

The next hour is spent preparing breakfast for the family. The men have to have a heavy meal before going to the fields. After that, she milks the cows, collects [firewood] or makes cow-dung cakes for fuel, tends the garden, cleans the cow shed, and dries the straw for burning.

By 9 a.m. she starts preparing the midday meal: grinding spices, peeling and cutting vegetables, and preparing the fish. Then she husks paddy [unmilled rice], winnows and sifts rice, and prepares rice products—popped rice, puffed rice, flat rice, or rice flour . . . .

Jute, paddy, and other [crops] for drying must be done when the sun shines.

After cooking she washes clothes, takes a bath, and bathes her children. Water has to be fetched from the river and the animals have to be fed. Sometimes she has to send the afternoon meal to the field, or if her husband is home she feeds him and the rest of the family. Only after everyone has eaten can she eat—usually only leftovers.

After lunch she weaves baskets, mats, makes quilts or *sikka* [rope hangers] for home use.

Since rural Bangladeshis usually have early supper, the woman has to start preparing the evening meal at 5 p.m. Two hours later, the evening meal is served.

In between these household chores, a rural wife would offer her prayers — five times a day.

And who wouldn't pray five times during such a day?

Perhaps it's no wonder that the greater longevity of women worldwide meets an exception in parts of developing Asia. In countries such as India, Pakistan, and Nepal, men on average outlive women.[5]

\* \* \*

Another telling social indicator is the small proportion of women, across much of Asia, who attend school or can read and write.

In India, for example, only 20 per cent of girls aged 12 to 17 are enrolled in school — about half the size of the male enrollment. In Pakistan, at the last national census there were two boys at primary school for every girl. In Papua New Guinea just 8 per cent of girls go to school, and in Bangladesh 6 per cent.[6]

The most rudimentary benefit of such education — basic literacy — is resultingly rare among Asian women, particularly in rural areas.

On the teeming Indian subcontinent and its environs (the countries of India, Bangladesh, Nepal, Pakistan, and Afghanistan), barely one or two women out of every 10 is literate. The literacy rate among men in scarcely a source of much national pride, either, but in the larger of these countries around half of men can read and write.[7]

But what use is literacy anyway to, say, the daughter of a poor Pakistani farmer? It is less important for its own sake, perhaps, than as a mind-set that equips a woman for the possibilities of a fuller life.

"Literacy is not only learning the alphabet. It is not an end in itself," says Yasmine Zahran, chief of UNESCO's Section of Equality of Educational Opportunity for Girls and Women. "It is the development of attitudes, skills, and support systems that are necessary if women are to succeed in their long march to equality and participation."[8]

\* \* \*

The most potent force keeping Asian women within the traditional confines of home and family may be economic.

Chronically high rates of both population growth and unemployment give the economies of most countries in the region enough of a challenge absorbing male job-seekers into the work force, without also having to cope with women. There simply isn't much work to be spread beyond the customary male breadwinners.

Here in Pakistan, a mere 2 per cent of women hold jobs.[9] In Bangladesh, they comprise just 5 per cent of industrial workers.[10] Even in so economically sophisticated a nation as India—one of the world's 10 most industrialized countries—only 14 per cent of women are gainfully employed.[11]

Up against such opposing pressures, it may be remarkable that there are as many working women in Asia as there are. Moreover, the proportion is increasing.

Asian women now make up more than half of the developing world's female labor force, according to the ILO.[12]

In nine countries in the region recently studied by the United Nations Economic and Social Commission for Asia and the Pacific (ESCAP), the female work force was expanding more rapidly than that of men in seven of them. In Thailand, the number of women with jobs outside the home had more than doubled in four years. In the Philippines, it had risen 10.4 per cent in three years.[13]

The fastest-growing category may be industrial workers. Asian women account for two-thirds of the sharp increase (by over 23 million) during the 1970s in the number of women throughout the developing world employed in industry, the ILO reports.

But these advances into the male domain of the workplace should be viewed in proper perspective.

Most women classified as workers in Asia are still unpaid family laborers, principally on farms.[14]

Those in the external labor market find themselves locked in an unequal—and usually futile—competition with their male fellow workers.

Women are generally overrepresented on the rolls of the unemployed (62 per cent of the jobless in the Philippines, for instance) and of temporary employees.[15]

And they tend to be confined to a narrow range of jobs traditionally reserved for women, frequently cast in a secondary or "helping" role to men.

In Malaysia, as an example, a statistical analysis of production workers lists 151 types of jobs for men, but only 33 for women. In four Asian capital cities—Bangkok, Jakarta, Manila, and Seoul—the largest number of employed women are domestic servants. Other leading occupations: sales clerks, waitresses, teachers, nurses, secretaries and other clerical workers.[16]

Wherever they work, women in Asia commonly find themselves "sedimented" to the bottom of the occupational hierarchy, and drawing lower wages than men doing comparable work.

This workplace sexism is all too familiar, of course, to their sisters in the

West, but on a less intimidating scale. American women, for one thing, now hold an outright majority of the country's professional jobs.[17]

Notwithstanding that one of them now heads their nation's government, Philippine women at last count filled only a quarter of the government civil service's 9,107 division chief positions. In the country's job market as a whole, for every peso earned by a man, a woman receives only 54 centavos. And the gap widens in rural areas, where every peso paid to a man is matched by a woman's 22 centavos.[18]

The mixed picture for women at work in Asia — bright daubs of progress peeking through encrusted layers of restrictions — is well illustrated by the case of Sri Lanka.

The tropical island nation stands out, in many ways, as one of the more congenial corners of the region for a woman. The schools are filled with more girls than boys (57 per cent of females aged 12 to 17, compared with 52 per cent of males), and 81 per cent of adult women are literate. Women make up 27 per cent of the work force, including a sizable share of some professions — more than a third of the country's doctors and dentists.

Yet the largest number of Sri Lankan working women are still found in the tea plantations, rice paddies, and other agricultural work sites. Only there have they achieved occupational equality, forming half the labor force.

It's an equality of the most menial sort. Plantation workers, for starters, are entitled to no paid medical leave or other time off, and just two public holidays a year.[19]

* * *

The welter of influences arrayed against female self-development in much of developing Asia is reinforced by something else, peculiarly Eastern: a cultural context, deeply ingrained over thousands of years, of customs and religions more overtly restrictive toward women than those under which Western women ever chafed.

The stifling institution of *purdah*, glimpsed here in northern Pakistan, survives in differing forms among adherents of both Islam and Hinduism, chiefly in rural areas, across vast tracts of the continent.

What the Koran has to say about the position of women is continually set forth as justification for a wide range of limitations imposed on females in the region's more fundamentalist Islamic nations. These teachings, among other things, prescribe modest dress for a woman to protect her purity, and devalue her testimony in a Muslim court of law (or *shariah*) as half that of a man.

(In some Islamic countries, including Pakistan, these narrow Koranic interpretations are just as tirelessly disputed by more "liberated" urban women.)

In East Asia, Confucian values tend to legitimize the concept that women ought to be submissive to men and live their lives passively at home.

The unhappy consequences are found in a country like South Korea. There women are still denied equal hereditary rights.[20]

And a large proportion of the nation's men even feel that they "own" their wives, according to a popular Korean women's magazine. As evidence, it cites the prevalence of wife-beating. A recent survey by the magazine disclosed that about half of Korean married women had been beaten by their husbands more than once.[21]

Such deep-rooted attitudes are slow to give way, but signs of change are visible in many parts of Asia.

A growing number of developing countries — running the cultural gamut from India to Malaysia to Fiji — now feel obliged to give women's equality at least lip service by enshrining the principle in their national constitutions.[22]

Ministries, agencies, and commissions on women's affairs have proliferated in recent years, along with private organizations.

Malaysia, despite stirrings of Islamic fundamentalism, has four women sitting in its cabinet, four deputy ministers, one ambassador, and (with a sex barrier broken in 1983) its first female judge.[23]

Even Confucian South Korea now has a woman cabinet minister, a government-run Korea Women's Development Institute, and a civil service that is one-fifth female (and growingly so).[24]

Earlier protections, meanwhile, are being updated. China has granted women equal rights in marriage since 1950 — one of the first "feudal" practices to be reformed by the incoming communist leadership. Liberalizations were incorporated in 1981. Since then, most of the country's divorces have been filed by women.[25]

In the end, the most effective spur to further emancipation may be, not high-flown rhetoric, but hard-headed recognition that freeing women from their traditional roles is a proven way of easing the pressure of population growth.

In Sri Lanka, among other places, the birthrate is falling as more women go out to work and postpone marriage. Sri Lankan women are now marrying five years later than they did 40 years ago — at 25, on average, rather than the tender age of 20 at which they wed in 1946.[26]

The long-time executive director of the United Nations Fund for Population Activities, the late Rafael M. Salas, has drawn the inescapable conclusion:

"An improvement in the status of women, by providing employment opportunities for them outside of traditional sectors, is considered important . . . for a decline in fertility rates."[27]

## INCHEON, SOUTH KOREA

A cigarette, a candy, or a newspaper can be bought in most any major city in Asia's developing countries by barely lifting a finger.

A wave of the hand or a nod of the head brings an army of street vendors scrambling to oblige.

At busy intersections, cars and buses stopped at traffic signals are swarmed by hawkers who materialize from the roadsides like ants at a picnic.

Innocent-eyed tots hoist tabloids with screaming headlines and lurid photos. Brash young men, cradling wooden boxes of smokes and candies in one arm, hop aboard buses. Others dart acrobatically among moving cars to sell a single cigarette to a motorist in a far lane.

The service rendered may be small, but the numbers involved are large. Something over 100 million vendors are estimated to ply the streets of developing Asia. And they are reckoned to generate between a fourth and a third of the total income produced in many cities.[1]

Since these hawkers have caught the attention of economists and social scientists—who term them, rather stuffily, the "informal sector" of the economy—more is known about them than their makeshift nature might suggest.

They are, to begin with, mostly young. A study by the International Labor Organization finds the average age of vendors in Manila to be 42, in Jakarta 36, and in Colombo 35. And the calling attracts up to half of all new entrants into urban work forces.

Vendors operate on the fringes of the economy. Little startup capital is required—often less than $100—and the returns are usually marginal. While collectively their income may be substantial, individually most earn less than the national minimum wage.[2]

Neither do they make much of a productive contribution to their nation's economy, nor perform what could be construed as an essential service. No one, after all, *needs* to have cigarettes brought to his car window.

But street vending does fill its economic niche. It provides income-producing work—however marginal—in a continent awash in surplus labor.

Four out of every 10 Asians of working age, according to the United Nations, are unemployed, underemployed, or grossly underpaid.[3]

* * *

Sun Jun Hwang knows a lot about street vendors. His father is one.

For 25 years he has witnessed the old man's financial struggles to rear a family of five sons (of whom he is the fourth) on the income squeezed from a small, streetside spice-and-condiment stall in Seoul.

Sun's genial face and grinning eyes — imparting an expression of perpetual whimsey — betray nothing of the hardships. But the hand-to-mouth upbringing has left him with a determination to find himself a more secure career. His ambition: to become an electrician.

Apart from his resolve, however, Sun would seem to have little else going for him. His only qualifications are a high school education and a stint of military service. He had no idea how to learn an electrician's trade, nor money to pay for it.

Then came a break. An elder brother told him about the government-run Vocational Training Institute here in Incheon.

Sun applied for admission, and although two to three applicants vie for each trainee position, was accepted.

Working hard at his one-year electrical course, in a blue uniform with his name stitched in yellow Korean ideograms above the left breast pocket, he seems destined to escape Asia's reservoir of idle and underused labor.

Graduation from one of South Korea's vocational training institutes is the nearest thing in this country to guaranteed employment.

They boast an impressive job-placement record. Roughly 90 per cent of the graduates find jobs within three months of finishing their course. Two-thirds of them are earning over twice the minimum wage for industrial workers.[4]

A survey among industrial employers found these graduates to be much sought-after.[5]

The key to their success may be that the institutes are patterned closely on the needs of local industry. They teach the skills for which there is a demand. And they emphasize practical training — in shops operating under factory conditions — over general and theoretical subjects.

The Incheon institute is plunked, fittingly, in the midst of an industrial area of this busy port city, surrounded by factories.

In its campus-like cluster of modernistic grey concrete buildings, 600 trainees pursue courses in carpentry, electrical work, electronics, foundry work, general machining, metal fitting, offset printing, and welding.

The trainees live, eight to a room, in dormitories. All are young men at this institute, although some women are enrolled at others.

Since the training is free, except for meals, it attracts a large proportion of low-income applicants, such as Sun.

One of his classmates in the electrical course, 25-year-old Jun Soo Im, is the orphaned son of a small farmer. His two elder brothers are common laborers. Another classmate, 19-year-old Jung Hyun Park, is the youngest son in a provincial farm family of seven children.

The Incheon institute is one of five established in the early 1970s. They have become the model for what has grown into an extensive system.

When the idea took shape, South Korea had only two vocational training institutions of acceptable standard, and the fast-industrializing country was rapidly developing a ravenous appetite for skilled manpower.

The five new institutes turned out about 2,500 graduates per year, but this output still met only a fraction of the demand. Another nine institutes soon followed, with a variety of foreign assistance. Eight more are now being built.

The success of South Korea's vocational training system may hold more than passing interest for other countries in the region wrestling with the chronic Asian problem of an oversupply of labor and a shortage of skills.

Indonesia, for example, is estimated to need an influx of 92,000 vocationally-skilled workers every year. Pakistan requires more than 26,000 a year; Singapore, over 21,000; the Philippines, 19,000.[6]

Like South Korea, other Asian nations are beginning to tap more fully the possibilities offered by vocational training. A total of $200 million is now being invested across the continent to upgrade such facilities.[7]

One country — Thailand — even has a vocational training program directed specifically at street vendors.

Some 200 young vendors, aged from 8 to 18, have been taken off the streets of Bangkok and given preparation for something more promising than hawking flowers or newspapers amid the traffic.[8]

## UJUNG PANDANG, INDONESIA

It was rather a shame when, a couple of years ago, they renamed this little seaport, known for centuries as Makassar.

An oil of the same name, extracted from the seeds of a local tree, slicked down the hair of countless Victorian men. And the cloth covers devised to protect the backs and arms of furniture — called "antimacassars" — have earned the town a permanent niche in the English language.

The disappearance of the name Makassar costs this chunk of the Indonesian archipelago probably its last link of familiarity with most of the English-speaking world.

Celebes—the island on which Ujung Pandang perches—is like that.

It, too, has undergone a name change. It's now Sulawesi.

And despite its flamboyant geography—shaped like a spinning pinwheel with four streamers twisting through 800 miles of ocean—it's an anonymous sort of place.

To most people, if they've heard of it at all, Celebes or Sulawesi is just one more underpopulated and underdeveloped island floating between two others: Borneo and New Guinea.

Since the Dutch subdued the enterprising spice traders, navigators, pirates, and local kings of Makassar 300 years ago, in fact, Sulawesi has attracted little in the way of either people or development.

Half again as large as Java, the seat of national government and the home of a majority of Indonesia's 170 million population, Sulawesi is inhabited by only one-tenth as many people.

Sulawesi's days of empty isolation, however, may be numbered. Acute overcrowding on islands such as Java is leading Indonesia to systematically resettle people to Sulawesi and other frontier areas, in what must surely be one of mankind's last great organized population movements.

* * *

Peter Fajans and Maman Odji, each in his own way, are part of this historic migration.

They are brought together here from backgrounds just about as dissimilar as one could imagine.

Mr. Fajans—more accurately, Dr. Fajans, M.D.—is a tall, lanky young American physician in wire-rimmed glasses from Ann Arbor, Michigan, where his father teaches at the University of Michigan medical school.

Having had difficulty choosing between a career in public health or anthropology, once he became a doctor he found work that combined both: conducting public-health research on the history-steeped Indonesian island of Bali.

Two years later, having acquired a fondness for Indonesians and facility in their language, Dr. Fajans became the public-health specialist on a team of American consultants for the resettlement program in southeast Sulawesi.

Maman Odji, one of the more than 50,000 "transmigrants" in this area, was drawn here for a much different reason: economic survival.

A slim-built farmer with bristly black hair, a droopy mustache, and an intent look in his eyes, he came here seven years ago from the Bandung region of Java. There he had been one of a family of 16 children eking out a living on a farm of less than 5 acres.

Crowded out of Java, he signed up as a 20th century pioneer in Sulawesi.

The island, about the size of the American state of Minnesota, is untamed tropical frontier. It is draped in a thick cloak of primary vegetation, from jagged green mountains, to rolling expanses of waist-deep *alang-alang* grass, to valleys of tangled rain forest.

Indigenous Sulawesians farm the land almost nomadically, hacking and burning away small fields and afterward abandoning them, while harvesting the starchy core of sago palms which throng the swamps.

Only jeeps and trucks—few cars—brave the punishing roads.

The southeastern arm of the island, one of Indonesia's emptiest quarters, is a place whose provincial capital (Kendari) had no electricity until five years ago, no telephone until three years ago, and still has no piped water system.

Maman Odji has survived Sulawesi's rigors. Now 40 years old and supporting a wife and three children on his 5-acre farm, he symbolizes many of the successes and shortcomings of Indonesia's ambitious transmigration program, in which both he and Dr. Fajans are now partners of sorts.

*Transmigrasi*, as it is known to Indonesians, has been going on since the Dutch rulers tried it in 1905. In the past 30 years more than 500,000 families or some 2.5 million persons have been relocated from teeming Java and the adjoining islands of Bali, Madura, and Lombok.[1] That's the rough equivalent of moving the population of Mississippi to, say, Alaska.

But the numbers invariably have fallen short of government targets, and many transmigrants have encountered unforeseen problems.

In the grassy settlement called Uepai where Maman Odji lives, 35 per cent of the initial families forsook their farms and moved back to Java or elsewhere.

They had been provided a generous resettlement package that included a simple wooden house and land, a one-year food allowance, and a three-year supply of seeds, fertilizer, and agrochemicals. It wasn't enough.

The undomesticated Sulawesi soil did not yield willingly to cultivation. Irrigation, draft animals, and proper farm implements were lacking. Conflicts arose with the local Sulawesians.

* * *

Problems such as these may be unavoidable, perhaps, in any undertaking so vast and complex as Indonesia's transmigration program.

Like the earlier peopling of other frontier areas elsewhere in the world—the American West, for example, or the Australian outback—transmigration amounts to a cultural and ecological invasion. And the resulting upheaval has brought its full share of challenges.

To the native inhabitants of the "outer islands" of Sulawesi, Borneo, Sumatra, and western New Guinea where transmigrants are moving in, the settlers from Java or Bali seem nearly as alien as did the homesteaders to the American Indians or the Australian farmers to the aborigines.

Although neighbors in the same archipelago, they differ in ethnic background, traditions, style of living, and frequently even language and religion. And the locals often resent all the free assistance extended to the uninvited newcomers.

Promoting a sense of nationalism within Indonesia's anthropological stew of cultures is, indeed, an avowed aim of transmigration.[2] But the government is sometimes accused of trying to "Javanize" the rest of the country by those who fear being reduced to minorities on their own islands.

Besides alien cultures, transmigration also imports alien cultivation.

Rice farming is what most of the transmigrants did back home on Java or Bali, and are expected to continue doing on their new farmsteads. But much of the land opened up for them turns out to be ill-suited for growing rice, or often little else either.

While the volcano-nourished soil on Indonesia's inner islands is among the richest in the world — one reason why they are so thickly populated — that on the outer islands tends to be rather light and infertile for most agriculture.

Merely subjecting it to cultivation often begins robbing the soil of whatever nutrients it has. Once stripped of its protective cover of vegetation and tilled, erosion and leaching quickly set in.[3]

Even in transmigration's most prosaic goal — reducing overpopulation in the inner islands — results have been less than spectacular. The number of people shipped out has been more than offset by natural population increase (of upwards of 1 million a year) in Java and Bali.

To critics, these shortcomings only confirm the wrongheadedness of the entire transmigration concept. They say the money — it costs several thousand dollars to resettle each family — might better be spent on family planning and developing job-creating industries.

But defenders view the problems as normal teething troubles to be smoothed out as experience is gained.

They argue that dispersing surplus population to underpopulated parts of the archipelago is a logical way of achieving a more even spread of both population and development.

Then there's the hard-to-quantify social benefit.

Most transmigrants are drawn from the ranks of the virtually resourceless.

In Java, the major supplier, seven out of every 10 farmers own no land at all or too little to feed their families.[4] No cost-effectiveness analysis can adequately measure the intangible value of giving to such a person a plot of land and a home.

* * *

Unmoved in its determination to keep moving people, Indonesia plans to relocate 3.7 million more by 1989.[5] Among them will be 19,000 additional families due here in southeast Sulawesi.

To transmigration veterans like Maman Odji and Peter Fajans, the preparations under way for the new arrivals suggest that lessons are being learned from the program's checkered past.

Rather than simply shipping in more newcomers, help also is being given to those already here. Community facilities — water supplies, schools, and roads — are being upgraded in 17 existing settlements of 5,900 earlier transmigrant families, such as Maman Odji's, and in 70 local villages of basket-like houses woven of split bamboo containing 26,000 indigenous Tolaki families.

Dr. Fajans is helping to set up a network of sorely-needed village health centers.

Nor are the transplanted Javanese and Balinese being left to fend for themselves quite so much agriculturally.

The new settlers will have irrigated cropland — some 22,700 acres of it — fed by the tawny waters of the jungle-lined Konaweha River. Each transmigrant family, new and old, will receive a draft animal and share the use of a plow, harrow, and harness.

Without such animal power, Maman Odji has been unable since coming here seven years ago to clear and cultivate half of his 5-acre allotment. A water buffalo or a head of Brahman or Bali cattle could as much as double the family income, and he is readying a corral and pasture in eager anticipation.

After early doubts and twinges of longing for his native Java, Maman Odji says he is glad he transmigrated.

He's not alone. His transmigration village, once decimated by dropouts, has filled all its vacancies, taken on 200 more families, and receives inquiries almost daily from persons interested in moving in.

On the crowded inner islands several hundred miles away across the Java Sea, the waiting lists of prospective transmigrants grow long.

If Indonesia's great population transfer experiment can be made to work here, then perhaps one day Sulawesi may be remembered for something besides Victorian hair oil.

## COLOMBO, SRI LANKA

Maligakanda Road slumbers peacefully in the wilting midday sun.

The white-walled postal substation is deserted, as is the tailor's shop across the way. Cars have relinquished the street to a lone, saffron-robed Buddhist priest shuffling along in sandals in the circle of shade cast by a black umbrella.

But the doorway to No. 73, next to the tailor's shop, opens onto a deafening clatter of activity. A printing press is stamping out the pages of a novel in curlicued Sinhalese script. Another is disgorging large sheets of uncut airmail envelopes.

Color portraits of the prime minister are stacked against the wall side-by-side with Sinhalese alphabet books for children and comic books about Sri Lanka's legendary first king.

Upstairs, three young artists hover over drawing-tables with illuminated, translucent tops, designing greeting cards for Christmas and *Vesak*, the Buddhist festive month.

Darting among the presses, the heaps of paper, and the din—keeping a proprietary eye on things—is a short, broad-beamed man with wiry, greying hair who looks more like a rough-hewn printer than the artist he really is.

H. A. Chandragupthe, who owns the firm which he calls *Lalithakalale* (meaning "fine arts"), studied art in neighboring India and made his living for 14 years as a self-employed commercial artist. He started out, like the young artists who now work for him, by designing greeting cards.

He expanded a few years ago from a one-man operation to a small employer, to the benefit not only of himself but of the needy Sri Lankan economy.

This, of course, is just the way that market forces are supposed to operate—parlaying individual initiative into economic growth. But it worked for Mr. Chandragupthe with the help of a financial tool sometimes regarded today as a foe of private enterprise: foreign aid.

Such aid is rather out of vogue just now in the capitals of some developed nations. It's argued that poorer countries might better be developed by private money, by the natural economic stimulation that occurs in a Western-style free market. "The magic of the marketplace," U.S. President Ronald Reagan fondly used to call it.[1]

But if Mr. Reagan would venture to Maligakanda Road and sit down with Mr. Chandragupthe in his crowded printing shop (if, that is, he could find room to sit!), he might make a disconcerting discovery: that in the world's developing lands, "the magic of the marketplace" often needs help to bring it off.

Like so many aspiring entrepreneurs in the capital-scarce Third World, Mr. Chandragupthe yearned to branch out but couldn't raise the necessary funds from commercial sources on terms he could afford.

His economic deliverance was a $48,836 loan from the Development Finance Corporation of Ceylon. The government-run DFCC lends money at interest rates several percentage points below commercial rates to promising enterprises with good prospects of helping develop this poor country (per capita gross national product: $285).

The DFCC gets its money from a variety of domestic and foreign sources. Mr. Chandragupthe's particular loan happened to come from $5 million in funds lent interest-free by the multinational Asian Development Bank from money contributed by 17 developed countries (including Mr. Reagan's).

Becoming one of the world's smaller foreign-aid recipients, he used the loan to buy an offset printer and a paper-trimming machine. Since then, business has boomed.

The little firm has become Sri Lanka's leading producer of greeting cards — 400,000 of them for *Vesak* and 200,000 for Christmas. Permanent jobs have been created for 15 employees, in a country where one of every six employable persons cannot find work. Five more employees will be squeezed into the 20-feet-wide shop when another new printing machine is delivered.

But the budding businessman who directs this thriving little empire still proudly thinks of himself, first and foremost, as a working artist. "The DFCC," as he rather poetically puts it, "gave the loan for my hands."

* * *

Tagor Sorman is a different kind of Asian businessman. He's a farmer.

That's an occupation which people don't instinctively associate with the business world, but in fact it comprises the continent's largest bloc of private-sector economic activity.

Asia — as, indeed, most of the rest of the globe outside of a relative handful of industrialized countries — is fundamentally a land of small, private farmers.

They, and those whom they employ, make up 50 to 90 per cent of the labor force in most of the region's developing countries; generate between 30 and 70 per cent of the gross domestic product; produce over one-third of the exports.[2]

Like businessmen everywhere, they survive economically on a combination of pluck, know-how, and native financial savvy. And 90 per cent of them do so with near-subsistence landholdings of less than 12 acres.[3]

Mr. Sorman—not his real name, which he was too embarrassed to give to a foreign visitor—farms four acres of swampland near Tulungagung in East Java, Indonesia.

The land here stretches flat, almost prostrate—painfully vulnerable to the volcanic eruptions that spew every 25 years or so from the snaggy green peak of Mt. Kelud on the northeast horizon, and to the regrettably more frequent floodings of the meandering Ngrowo River. This is one of the poorest yet most populous corners of Indonesia.

All his life, the tall, spare grandfather with a traditional black *peci* cap atop his grey-haired head, watched helplessly as the rising river waters repeatedly invaded his rice plot (and house) during the six rainy months of the year.

The inundations had condemned Mr. Sorman's family of five, and virtually all the other 41,000 farm families in the flood area, to scratch out a living below the national household poverty line of about $385 a year.

No "magic of the marketplace" performed its economic legerdemain for these struggling entrepreneurs. The private sector, after all, rarely builds public works. And a major flood-control project was needed to halt the deluges and lift the farmers out of poverty.

Various dams, canals, and floodways have been tried over the past 40 years by the government and the inundated residents themselves. Mr. Sorman and his fellow farmers recently turned their own shovels to the task of digging a 12-mile-long canal. The floods have subsided somewhat.

The job of stanching them once and for all has fallen, as so often, to the financier of last resort: foreign aid.

A package of $47 million in loans and grants from various international donors is funding a network of flood-control facilities that will drain the river's overflow harmlessly away through a tunnel into the Indian Ocean.

Construction is still going on, but already Mr. Sorman is rejoicing over the first unflooded, two-crop season (rice and corn) of his long life. Other farmers fortunate enough to have irrigation are even reaping three crops a year.

Thousands of small farmer-businessmen are getting a taste of financial success, and the economy of this impoverished region of Java is gaining a new class of prospering entrepreneurs.

\* \* \*

Foreign aid is no cure-all for Asia's development needs, any more than are market forces.

Each has demonstrated that it performs certain aspects of the job quite capably, but other aspects less well—or not at all.

The economic Darwinism of the marketplace imposes incentives for the needy to help themselves, and enforces a measure of efficiency. But the pursuit of profits is hardly a reliable guide for all the varied economic decisions that arise in developing a poor country, and frequently produces very wrong choices indeed.

Nonfood crops are grown for export instead of food crops needed to feed the local populace. People at an early stage of development are introduced consumer products which they neither need nor can afford. Drugs and pesticides banned as unsafe in industrialized nations are palmed off on the unwitting Third World.[4]

Foreign aid, on the other hand, better lends itself to targeting toward genuine development needs. But it can foster dependence, and often must be filtered through a bureaucratic process that swathes it in paperwork, forces it into a stereotyped mold, and lifts it out of touch with local conditions.

The annals of foreign-aid projects are peppered with factories cranking out products for which there are no markets; hydroelectric dams that waterlog surrounding cropland; multi-faceted agricultural projects too complicated for the local farmers to run.[5]

But if salvation is unlikely to be found exclusively in either economic course, neither is foreign aid necessarily inimical to a free market.

Aid can stimulate growth in the private sector of an economy when market forces fall short (as in the case of the Sri Lankan printer) or through areas of economic activity traditionally reserved for the public sector (as with the flood-stricken Indonesian farmer).

No less staunchly capitalistic an institution than the Organization for Economic Cooperation and Development (OECD)—an entity of nearly all the world's industrialized "free market" countries—has conceded that private investment "tends to bypass the basic development needs of the poorest countries, where there is no immediate profit."[6]

In some developing countries, the marketplace is either nonexistent or so small as to be inconsequential. These range from nations where private economic activity is restricted for ideological reasons, such as Burma, to those where it is stifled by sheer poverty, such as Bangladesh.

If an economy is peopled largely by self-sufficient, subsistence farmers or indigents surviving on a few hundred dollars a year—as in much of developing Asia—the concept of a Western-style free market remains something of a misnomer. It's a "market" that few consumers have money to patronize, and that few private investors, either domestic or foreign, find very inviting.

In such places, rhetoric about "the magic of the marketplace" holds little enchantment.

A recent finance minister of Bangladesh, Saifur Rahman, observes acidly that his dirt-poor country has "not yet been taken as a desirable suitor" by free-market financiers. Its one-sided trade with Western markets, meanwhile, only produces deficits that drive the nation ever deeper into debt.

"The market smiles at the rich," he says, "but frowns upon the poor."[7]

# Notes

## INTRODUCTION

1. A study by the United Nations Educational, Scientific, and Cultural Organization (UNESCO), cited by Wilbur Schramm and Erwin Atwood, *Circulation of News in the Third World: A Study of Asia* (Hong Kong: The Chinese University Press, 1981), p. 189.

2. Figure provided to the author by Mrs. Alice Villadolid of the *Times*, Manila, July 1983.

3. Letter to the author from Gannett Executive Vice-President John C. Quinn, 2 August 1983.

4. Rosemary Righter, *Whose News? Politics, the Press and the Third World* (London: Andre Deutsch Ltd., 1978), p. 80.

5. *Ibid.*

6. Former UPI Vice-President Roger Tatarian, cited by Philip C. Horton, ed., *The Third World and Press Freedom* (New York: Praeger, 1978), p. 41.

7. Schramm and Atwood, *Circulation of News in the Third World.*

8. Benjamin A. Batson, *The End of Absolute Monarchy in Siam* (New York: Oxford University Press, 1985).

9. Cited by Richard Critchfield, *Villages* (Garden City, N.Y.: Anchor Press/Doubleday, 1983), p. 197.

10. *Asian Drama: An Inquiry Into the Poverty of Nations*, abridged ed. (New York: Random House, 1972), pp. 209–210.

## MAKING ENOUGH MONEY TO LIVE

### RASAU KERTEH, MALAYSIA

Portions of this chapter previously appeared in *Development Forum* (New York), *The Asian Wall Street Journal* (Hong Kong), and *Business Ventures* (Manila) in 1982 and 1983.

1. *World Development Report, 1980* (Washington: International Bank for Reconstruction and Development, 1980), p. 32.

2. Based on per capita gross national product.

3. Basic federal minimum wage in effect in 1988.

4. World Bank, *World Development Report, 1980*, p. 33.

5. Speech by S.A.M.S. Kibria, executive secretary of the United Nations Economic and Social Commission for Asia and the Pacific (ESCAP), reported by Agence France Presse (hereafter cited as AFP) from Bangkok, 13 January 1982.

6. Various reports of the Asian Development Bank (hereafter cited as ADB).

7. U.S. Motor Vehicle Manufacturers Association, cited in "The Making of a Motor Car," *Asiaweek* (Hong Kong), 28 September 1984.

8. UNESCO report, cited in "Asia-Pacific Region Major Seat of Illiteracy," *The Bangladesh Observer* (Dhaka), 23 October 1983.

9. World Health Organization study, reported in "The Price of Life," *The Rising Nepal* (Kathmandu), 28 October 1983.

10. ADB, *Basic Facts: DMCs of ADB*, April 1983. (DMCs is abbreviation for developing member countries.)

## BATURAJA, INDONESIA

A portion of this chapter previously appeared in *The Asian Wall Street Journal* in 1982.

1. Reported by Reuters from Bangkok, 3 September 1981.

2. Figures from ESCAP conference, cited in "Urban population to grow by 700m," *The Bangladesh Observer*, 5 October 1982.

3. *Ibid.*

4. *Ibid.*

5. "Bombay: The Darker Side of Success," *Asiaweek*, 4 May 1984.

6. "Urban Development in the Philippines," *The Bank's World* (a publication of the World Bank), September 1982.

7. "A sprawling, thirsty giant," *Far Eastern Economic Review* (Hong Kong)(hereafter cited as *Review*), 29 March 1984.

8. Shiomo Angel *et al.*, *Land for Housing the Poor* (Singapore: Select Books, 1983), book review, *Review*, 9 June 1983.

9. ESCAP report cited in note 1 above.

10. Reported in "The roots of the problem," *Review*, 11 September 1981.

## ASAU, WESTERN SAMOA

1. ESCAP, ADB, and South Pacific Bureau for Economic Cooperation, *Industrial Survey of the South Pacific*, June 1983, p. 19, table 5 in regional report.

2. *Ibid.*, p. 4 in country study for Western Samoa.

3. *Ibid.*, p. 22 in country study for Western Samoa.

4. *World Development Report, 1983* (Washington: International Bank for Reconstruction and Development, 1983), pp. 152–153, table 3.

5. Seiji Naya, "Small-Scale Industries in Asian Economic Development: Problems and Prospects," *ADB Economics Office Report Series*, No. 24 (February 1984).

6. "Cottage Industry's Role Predominant in Nepal," *The Rising Nepal*, 26 July 1981.

7. World Bank, *World Development Report, 1983*, pp. 188–189, table 21.

8. *Ibid.*

9. "India: A return to rural capitalism," *Business Week*, 11 June 1979.

## SEOUL, SOUTH KOREA

1. World Bank, *World Development Report, 1983*, box 7.3.
2. "30 Years Later: Seoul's Half-Miracle," *The New York Times*, 9 August 1983.
3. See note 1 above.
4. ADB, *Country Program Paper*, March 1984.
5. ADB sources.

# GETTING ENOUGH FOOD TO EAT

## ASHUGANJ, BANGLADESH

A portion of this chapter previously appeared in the *Far Eastern Economic Review* in 1982.

1. ADB, *Appraisal Report, Second Livestock Project (Bangladesh)*, November 1984.
2. "Bangladesh Hunger Linked to Feudal System," *The New York Times*, 24 November 1981.
3. *Ibid.*
4. See note 1 above.
5. "Hungry Bangladesh Threatens to Burst Its Seams," *The New York Times*, 6 April 1983.
6. WHO report, cited in "WHO notes problem of obesity," *Bulletin Today* (Manila), 2 November 1984.
7. Statement by Maurice Williams, executive director of World Food Council at conference in Manila, reported by AFP, 24 February 1983.
8. Statement by S.A.M.S. Kibria, executive secretary of ESCAP, reported by AFP from Bangkok, 12 January 1982.
9. See note 7 above.
10. U.S. Department of Agriculture statistics, reported in *International Herald Tribune* (Hong Kong), 2 March 1983, tables.
11. ADB, *Agriculture* (undated booklet).
12. Harry T. Oshima, Paper No. 21, *ADB Economics Staff Papers*, p. 60 (footnote 4).
13. International Rice Research Institute figure, cited in "Los Baños-developed new rice varieties seen as Asia's green revolution hope," *Times Journal* (Manila), 20 July 1982.
14. *World Development Report, 1983*, pp. 158–159, table 6.
15. *Ibid.* and *The World Almanac and Book of Facts, 1986* (New York: Newspaper Enterprise Association, 1985), p. 157.
16. Estimate of United Nations Fund for Population Activities, reported in "10,000 babies being born every day," *The Bangladesh Observer*, 4 October 1983.
17. World Bank study, reported in "Land Reform Only Way Out for Bangladesh," *The Bangladesh Observer*, 1 April 1983.
18. Pilot agricultural census published by Bangladesh Bureau of Statistics, reported in "Irrigation coverage up, cropping density down," *The Bangladesh Times* (Dhaka), 5 March 1984.
19. *Ibid.*

20. ADB project reports and economic memoranda.

21. See note 14 above.

22. ADB reports.

## TALUNGAGUNG, INDONESIA

1. " 'Yes' and 'No' in Indonesia's food self-sufficiency," *The Indonesia Times* (Jakarta), 20 July 1982.

2. "Running to stand still," *Review*, 28 August 1981.

3. World Bank, *World Development Report, 1983*, p. 158, table 6.

4. See note 2 above, and "ASEAN Agriculture Maintains Momentum," *The Bangladesh Observer*, 28 January 1984.

5. See note 1 above.

6. "Problems of plenty," *Review*, 7 November 1985, and Reuters report from Jakarta, 20 February 1983.

7. ADB, *Appraisal Report, Technical Assistance for Secondary Food Crops Development Project (Indonesia)*, July 1984.

8. "Rice Crop Changes Indonesia's Fortunes," *The Asian Wall Street Journal*, 21 November 1984.

9. Announcement by State Logistic Board *(Bulog)*, reported by AFP from Jakarta, 8 December 1981.

10. Reported by Reuters from Jakarta, 20 February 1983.

11. *Ibid.*

12. "Problems of plenty."

13. Government announcement, cited in "Indonesia now has world's biggest stockpile of rice," *Bulletin Today*, 27 January 1985.

14. Reported in "Asia's food output surpasses population growth," *The Economic Times* (Bombay), 8 December 1983.

15. V. S. Vyas, "Asian Agriculture: Achievements and Challenges," *Asian Development Review* (Manila), vol. 1, no. 2 (1983).

16. International Rice Research Institute statistics and ADB reports; see also note 13, preceding chapter.

17. Statement by Philippines Ministry of Agriculture and Food, November 1984.

18. Statement of Kunio Takase, deputy director of Agriculture and Rural Development Department, at ADB senior staff meeting, 10 February 1982.

19. "Global Efforts Cultivate Rice Development in Asia," *The Asian Wall Street Journal*, 10 April 1984 (excerpts of an article by M. S. Swaminathan, director of the International Rice Research Institute, in *Scientific American*, January 1984).

20. M. S. Swaminathan, "The Rice Race," *Global Futures Digest*, spring 1983.

21. *Ibid.* and see note 13, preceding chapter.

22. ADB, *Appraisal Report, Technical Assistance for International Irrigation Management Institute*, October 1983, and other ADB reports.

23. "Eastern Promise," *The Economist Development Report* (London), May 1984.

24. "IDA Cuts Could Spawn Disastrous Consequences," *Journal of Commerce* (New York), 27 October 1983, and "India fulfills food prediction, but starvation hasn't gone away," *Star & Tribune* (Minneapolis), 25 January 1983.

25. See note 18 above.

26. "The seeds of a glut," *Review*, 29 August 1985.

27. *Ibid.*

28. "China goes to market," *Review*, 13 December 1984.

29. "A success story so far, but new efforts are needed," *Review*, 20 March 1986.

30. *Ibid.* and see note 28 above.

31. "The turning point," *Review*, 24 January 1985.

32. Qutubuddin Aziz, information minister, Embassy of Pakistan, London, in letter to *International Herald Tribune*, 6 December 1983.

33. "Economic husbandry," *Review*, 31 January 1985.

34. ADB, *Appraisal Report, Irrigation Sector Project (Philippines)*, November 1983.

35. Article dispatched by AFP from Rangoon, 15 June 1982.

36. "Feeding on the past," *Review*, 15 August 1985.

37. See note 35 above.

38. See, for example, "India fulfills;" "Anxiety as food production fails to keep pace," *Financial Times* (London), 8 February 1982; "Millions Hungry as Philippines Exports Food," *The Washington Post*, 30 October 1980; "Death haunts island's cradles of hunger," *The Guardian* (London), 26 September 1986.

## SAMUT SAKORN, THAILAND

1. ADB, *Appraisal Report, Aquaculture Development Project (Thailand)*, November 1978.

2. Food and Agriculture Organization estimate, cited in "Under-paid, second-class citizens—that's fishermen," *Review*, 2 August 1984.

3. See note 1 above.

4. ADB figure.

5. See note 2 above.

6. ADB, *Appraisal Report, Regional Technical Assistance for Aquaculture Research and Training*, September 1982.

7. "Fish for food and fun," *The Bangladesh Observer*, 21 December 1982.

8. "Cage culture of fish," *Daily News* (Colombo), 1 February 1983.

9. "Can earth's waters be an answer to food shortage?" *Daily News*, 27 January 1983.

10. Reported by AFP from Kota Kinabalu, 9 January 1983.

11. See note 6 above.

12. "High-Yield Fish-Farming," *Michigan Today*, December 1985.

# WHERE ESSENTIALS OF LIFE ARE LUXURIES

## KALUDHER, PAKISTAN

1. *Asian Electric Power Utilities Data Book* (Manila: ADB, 1983), pp. 11–12, and "In Search of Energy for Rural Asia's Billions," *The Asian Wall Street Journal*, 16 December 1981.

2. "Solar electric power for the villages," *Daily News*, 28 January 1982.

3. ADB, *Basic Facts: DMCs of ADB*, April 1986.

4. ADB figures.

5. ILO study, reported in "Myths and Realities of Rural Electrification," *The Bangladesh Observer*, 1 March 1984.

6. "Rural electrification," *Dawn* (Karachi), 6 January 1984.

## BANGKOK, THAILAND

1. ADB, *Appraisal Report, Second Bangkok Water Supply Project (Thailand)*, December 1979, and "Bangkok: 200 Years of Triumph and Tribulation," *Asiaweek*, 23 April 1982.

2. ADB, *Appraisal Report*, and survey by Asian Institute of Technology, reported in "That sinking feeling," *Review*, 25 June 1982.

3. "Urban Development in the Philippines."

4. Karachi Development Authority figures, reported in "Karachi likely to be a city of 15m by 2000," *Business Recorder* (Karachi), 9 November 1982.

5. "Jakarta population explosion," *Business Times* (Singapore), 22 June 1983; "A sprawling, thirsty giant;" "Salt in the wounds," *The Guardian*, 26 September 1986.

6. ADB figures.

7. Statement by Marten Schalekamp, chairman of International Congress on Water Distribution, reported by AFP from Zurich, 6 September 1982.

8. Designated by the United Nations in 1978.

## NUKU'ALOFA, TONGA

1. ADB figures.

2. United Nations figures, reported in "How the World Can Become Smaller?" *The Bangladesh Observer*, 6 January 1983.

3. "Instrument fault causes 40% of wrong numbers," *Review*, 6 September 1984, and "Telephone: The Overlooked Medium," *The Bangladesh Observer*, 10 June 1984.

4. ADB figure.

5. Reported by Reuters from Rangoon, 20 December 1982.

6. Reported by AFP from Tokyo, 21 February 1984.

7. "Private squalor and public lives," *The Guardian*, 23 February 1985 (reprinted from *The Washington Post*).

8. "Modern phone system up," *Bulletin Today*, 2 February 1985.

9. "Who Owns the Telephones?" *Asiaweek*, 26 August 1983, and author's experience.

10. "Telephone tangle," *Review*, 18 October 1984.

11. "Instrument fault" and "The Telephone: Vital Instrument of Economic Development," *ADB Quarterly Review*, July 1986.

12. See note 10 above.

13. Author's experience.

14. "The Telephone."

15. "Instrument fault."

16. See note 2 above.

17. "A switched-off service," *Review*, 19 July 1984.

18. See note 2 above.

19. "The small screen is still a distant vision for the majority in India," *Review*, 21 June 1984.

20. "A space-age system spreads the word to the villagers," *Review*, 1 March 1984, and ADB, *Basic Facts* (see chap. Kaludher, Pakistan, note 3).

21. Reported by Reuters from Colombo, 15 February 1982.

22. Reported by Reuters from Rangoon, 2 February 1983.

23. Reported by AFP from Beijing, 15 March 1984.

24. "Indian TV: Weighing Development Against Entertainment," *International Herald Tribune*, 6 July 1984.

25. Government economic planning survey, reported in "Japanese consumerism," *The Korea Herald* (Seoul), 25 May 1984.

26. *The World Almanac*, pp. 549, 568; report in *The Statesman* (Calcutta), 30 April 1984; ADB figures.

27. Published daily broadcasting schedules, 1981, and report by AP-Dow Jones from Dhaka, 20 February 1984.

## KATHMANDU, NEPAL

1. ADB, *Appraisal Report, Paper Mill Technical Services Project (Nepal)*, December 1982.

2. "The might of the pen," *Review*, 26 December 1985.

3. "Books too expensive? Then copy your own," *Review*, 7 November 1985.

4. Observations of Goh Keng Swee, first deputy prime minister of Singapore, in "Eldecia's long road to success," *Review*, 1 December 1983 (based on lecture at Royal Society, London).

5. Myrdal, *Asian Drama*, p. 398.

6. Figures from World Congress on Books and UNESCO, cited in "The Book Industry," *The Rising Nepal*, 27 February 1983.

7. "Pakistan's people wake up suddenly to a frightening education gap," *Review*, 12 April 1984.

8. See note 2 above.

9. ADB figure.

10. See note 2 above.

11. "Multitudinous voices," *Review*, 18 July 1985.

12. "An industry in better shape than ever before," *Review*, 1 March 1984.

13. See note 6 above.

14. See note 1 above.

# EVERYDAY ENERGY AND ENVIRONMENTAL CRISES
## BRAHMANBARIA, BANGLADESH

A portion of this chapter previously appeared in the *New Zealand Herald* (Auckland) in 1984.

1. Libby Bassett, ed., *World Environment Report, 1983* (New York: World Environment Center, 1983).

2. ADB, *Asian Electric Power Utilities Data Book*, p. 25.

3. Speech by F. Mahtab, Bangladesh minister for planning, in Osaka, reported by *Mainichi Shimbun* (Tokyo), 7 October 1981.

4. ADB estimate.

5. ADB, *Appraisal Report, Natural Gas Development Project (Bangladesh)*, December 1980.

6. *Asian Energy Problems: An Asian Development Bank Survey* (New York: Praeger, 1982), pp. 195–198, 228–238.

7. ESCAP estimate, reported in "Efforts to Diversify Energy Sources," *The Bangladesh Observer*, 27 October 1983.

8. Figures on development of the country's gas resources are drawn from an interview by the author with F. K. Khilji, managing director of Sui Gas Transmission Co. Ltd., December 1982 in Karachi, and *Energy Year Book, 1981* (Islamabad: Pakistan Directorate General of Energy Resources, 1981).

9. See note 6 above.

10. ADB, *Post-Evaluation Report, Multi-Project Loan (Tonga)*, undated.

## KATHMANDU, NEPAL

1. *Small Is Beautiful: Economics As If People Mattered* (New York: Harper & Row, 1975).

2. "In Search of Energy" (see chap. Kaludher, Pakistan, note 1).

3. *Ibid.* and "Big energy supplies from little dams," *Dawn*, 20 October 1984.

4. See chap. Janakpur, Nepal.

## SEOUL, SOUTH KOREA

1. Reported by AFP from Seoul, 9 March 1984.

2. "Too big for its own good," *Review*, 3 May 1984, and "Rural population moves to cities leaving dearth of local workers," *The Korea Herald*, 27 May 1984.

3. *Country Program Paper* (see earlier chap. Seoul, South Korea, note 4).

4. *Ibid.* and "A smell of success in the battle against pollution," *Review*, 18 July 1985.

5. "Private squalor" (see chap. Nuku'alofa, Tonga, note 7).

6. ESCAP study, reported in "U.N. Study Says Fast-Growing Asia Faces Major Environmental Damage," *The Washington Post*, 30 March 1982.

7. *Ibid.*

8. Dr. Meizar Syafei, private environmentalist, cited by Reuters from Jakarta, 3 August 1983.

9. "Calcutta now a dying city," *The Bangladesh Observer*, 2 April 1982, and "Bombay: The Darker Side of Success," *Asiaweek*, 4 May 1984.

10. UNEP estimates, reported in "Development Takes Heavy Toll in Asia," *The Bangladesh Observer*, 1 January 1984.

11. See note 6 above.

12. "Saving China's Birds," *Audubon*, November 1985. Mr. Li was elevated to premier in 1987.

13. "Indonesia manages its environment," *The IDRC Reports* (Ottawa), April 1984. (IDRC is abbreviation for International Development Research Centre.)

14. "Ganga to be cleansed of temporal pollution," *Review*, 12 December 1985, and " 'River of poison' threatens India," *Bangkok Post*, 21 February 1982.

15. "A slow stirring of environmental concern," *Review*, 19 December 1985.

16. Reported by UPI from Kathmandu, 25 June 1984. It is known as the King Mahendra Trust for Nature Conservation.

17. See note 15 above.

18. Environmental Preservation Law, enacted December 1977.

19. ADB, *Appraisal Report, Han River Basin Environmental Master Plan Project (Korea)*, September 1981.

20. Statistics on southern Thailand are extracted from ADB, *Appraisal Report, Songkhla Lake Basin Planning Study (Thailand)*, November 1982.

## JANAKPUR, NEPAL

1. Reported in ADB documents.

2. FAO survey, reported in "Asian Forest Resources Ravaged at Alarming Rate," *The Rising Nepal*, January 1982.

3. ESCAP study (see preceding chap., note 6).

4. See note 2 above; "How to Save Asia's Forests?" *Asiaweek*, 13 July 1984; proceedings of United Nations conference, reported by Reuters from Geneva, 19 November 1981.

5. See note 2 above.

6. "The petrified forests," *Review*, 20 August 1982.

7. Reported by Reuters from Rome, 6 November 1983.

8. Reported by AFP from New Delhi, 6 March 1984.

9. See note 2 above.

10. See note 7 above.

11. Proceedings of UN conference, cited in note 4 above.

12. ADB figures.

13. Reported in *The Rising Nepal*, 20 July 1984.

14. An incident in 1983 in Karnataka. See "Trees for the People," *The Sunday Statesman* (Calcutta), 4 December 1983.

# PHYSICAL AND INTELLECTUAL NOT-SO-WELL-BEING
## ANGORAM, PAPUA NEW GUINEA

A portion of this chapter previously appeared in *Pacific Islands Monthly* (Sydney) in 1984.

1. $213.4 million for food *vs.* $248.4 million for petroleum in 1981 (18.3 per cent *vs.* 21.3 per cent of all import commodities), according to ADB, *Country Notes on Papua New Guinea*, August 1983.

2. R. Gerard Ward and Andrew Proctor, eds., *South Pacific Agriculture: Choices and Constraints* (Canberra: Australian National University Press, 1980), p. 42.

3. *Ibid.*, pp. 333–334.

4. ADB figure.

5. ADB, *Basic Facts*, and World Bank, *World Development Report, 1980*, table 1 (see chap. Rasau Kerteh, Malaysia, notes 1, 10).

6. *Ibid.*, table 22.

7. ADB, *Basic Facts*, and figures reported in *The Rising Nepal*, 21 February 1984.

8. WHO study, reported in "The Price of Life," *The Rising Nepal*, 28 October 1983.

9. WHO figures in ADB documents.

10. *World Development Report, 1980*, table 22.

11. *Ibid.* and chap. Bangkok, Thailand.

12. A study conducted in Gujarat, reported in "Sick Lungs," *The Rising Nepal*, 13 January 1984.

13. ADB, *Basic Facts*.

14. *Ibid.*

## MANILA, PHILIPPINES

1. Gerald M. Daigler, *Living in the Philippines* (Manila: The American Chamber of Commerce of the Philippines, 1980), p. 22.

2. Cited in "The non-Chinese syndrome," *Review*, 22 March 1984.

3. James R. Roach, ed., *India 2000: The Next Fifteen Years* (Riverdale, Md.: The Riverdale Co., Inc., 1986), pp. 138–139, and "Hindi fails to replace English," *Business Recorder*, 21 April 1983.

4. 1971 national census (last for which language statistics available), reported in "Hindi fails."

5. *Ibid.* and world language figures compiled by Center for Applied Linguistics, cited in *Webster's New International Dictionary*, 1982 ed., p. 641.

6. "Hindi fails."

7. "India's anthem: was it chance or providence?" *Review*, 31 October 1985.

8. "State maintains tight grip on broadcasting," *Review*, 18 July 1985.

9. "Islands of modern technology in a sea of backwardness," *Review*, 18 July 1985.

10. "Multitudinous voices" (see initial chap. Kathmandu, Nepal, note 11).

11. "Hindi fails."

12. See, for example, daily broadcasting schedule in *Business Recorder*, 26 January 1984.

13. ADB sources.

14. D. J. Matthews, C. Shackle, and S. Husain, *Urdu Literature* (London: Third World Foundation, 1985), book review, *Review*, 2 January 1986.

15. James Morris, *Farewell the Trumpets: An Imperial Retreat* (London: Penguin Books, 1978), p. 486.

16. "In the name of jihad," *Review*, 9 January 1986.

17. "Class war fare," *The Guardian*, 26 April 1985.

18. "A problem of credibility," *Review*, 19 September 1985.

19. "Urdu being adopted gradually in all spheres of life," *Business Recorder*, 24 October 1984.

20. World language figures, cited in note 5 above.

21. Announcement by Education Minister Majeed Khan, reported by Reuters from Dhaka, 27 January 1983.

22. Reported by Reuters from Dhaka, 20 February 1984.

23. "Legacy of Language," 30 May 1984.

24. Statement at opening of parliament, reported by Reuters from Colombo, 9 February 1983.

25. "The dilemma of unifying a multilingual society," *Review*, 17 November 1983.

26. *Ibid.*

27. Statement at public reception, reported by Reuters from Singapore, 18 February 1984.

28. See note 2 above.

29. *Ibid.*

30. Lee statement, cited in note 27 above.

31. "Bringing order to the Pacific babel," *Pacific Islands Monthly*, June 1984.

32. *Ibid.*

33. P. 410 (see introduction, note 10).

34. Figures from World Congress on Books and UNESCO (see initial chap. Kathmandu, Nepal, note 6).

35. Nationally broadcast address by president, reported in "Introduce Bangla in all walks of life: Ershad," *The Bangladesh Observer*, 31 January 1983.

36. See note 25 above and IBM advertisement, *Review*, 22 May 1986.

37. Myrdal, *Asian Drama* (see introduction, note 10), p. 409.

38. Quoted, *ibid.*

39. *Ibid.*, p. 410.

40. UNESCO report (see chap. Rasau Kerteh, Malaysia, note 8).

41. ADB, *Basic Facts* (see chap. Kaludher, Pakistan, note 3).

42. A study conducted at the university in 1979, reported in "Hong Kong School System Troubled by Language Problem," *International Herald Tribune*, 16 May 1984.

# HARNESSING HUMAN RESOURCES

## MANILA, PHILIPPINES

1. "Migration Changes Map of ME," *The Bangladesh Observer*, 18 September 1984 (reprinted from *Arab News* [London]).

2. "Gulf states trying to reduce dependence on foreign labor," *The Bangladesh Observer*, 22 April 1984.

3. "The pipeline runs dry," *Review*, 13 September 1984, and "10pc of total force working abroad," *Business Recorder*, 22 June 1984.

4. See note 1 above.

5. Philippine Overseas Employment Administration figures, reported in "Filipino Women Workers Major Dollar Earners," *The Bangladesh Observer*, 30 January 1984, and "Wages tip the balance," *Review*, 27 September 1984.

6. "A Gulf well runs dry," *Review*, 3 March 1983.

7. "Saudi ladies do have more money and fun," *Review*, 17 October 1985.

8. Bangladesh: 227,487, reported in "Manpower Export at a Glance," *The Bangladesh Observer*, 9 May 1984. South Korea: 183,000, cited in note 1 above.

9. Estimate of Manpower Minister Sudomo, reported by Reuters from Jakarta, 4 October 1983.

10. "China takes world's unwanted jobs," *Business Times*, 5 June 1984 (reprinted from *The New York Times*).

11. ILO findings, reported in "The Ebbing Tide of Migrant Outflow," *The Bangladesh Observer*, 16 November 1984.

12. Study prepared by ILO for Pakistan Ministry of Labor, reported in "The pipeline" (note 3 above).

13. Commerce industry computation, reported by AP-Dow Jones from Bangkok, 23 January 1984.

14. "Wages tip" (note 5 above).

15. See note 11 above, and "Manpower exports in bulk: a nightmare for future economic management," *Dawn*, 6 February 1983.

16. See note 6 above.

17. A study by the United Nations Fund for Population Activities, reported in "Cheap Labour," *The Rising Nepal*, 10 July 1983.

18. World Bank, *World Development Report, 1983* (see chap. Talungagung, Indonesia, note 3), p. 105.

19. Interviews by the author, and see note 6 above.

20. Reported in "Wages tip" (note 5 above).

21. Philippine Overseas Employment Administration figures, cited in note 5 above.

22. See note 7 above.

23. See note 2 above.

24. Statement of Pakistan interior minister, reported in *Business Recorder*, 13 April 1983.

25. Reported in "More ME Jobs for Bangladeshis," *The Bangladesh Observer*, 14 February 1984.

26. Reported by Reuters from Geneva, 22 November 1983.

27. See note 2 above.

28. "Gulf Countries Worried About Migrant Workers," *The Rising Nepal*, 30 October 1982.

29. See note 6 above.

30. Reported by AFP from Paris, 7 November 1982.

31. "More levy on foreign maids in Singapore likely," *The Bangladesh Observer*, 1 October 1984, and report by AFP from Singapore, 14 October 1984.

32. See note 6 above.

33. See note 12 above.

34. See note 2 above.

35. See note 12 above.

## NEAR PESHAWAR, PAKISTAN

1. "Child wives of Bangladesh," *People* (London), vol. 12, no. 3 (1985).

2. International Planned Parenthood Federation, *Women in the Commonwealth* (chart), 1985.

3. Statement by Minister for Population and Environment Emil Salim, reported by AP from Jakarta, 6 March 1984.

4. Shahana Alamgir, "Bangladesh rural women's contributions often ignored," *The Indonesia Times*, 30 October 1984 (from Depthnews syndicate).

5. A survey by World Priorities, cited in "Women's power," *People*, vol. 12, no. 3 (1985).

6. See note 2 above.

7. See note 2 above, and ESCAP studies, reported in "Long Way from Equality," *The Rising Nepal*, 12 November 1984.

8. "Educating girls: progress and sexual prejudice," *People*, vol. 12, no. 2 (1985).

9. ADB figure.

10. "The choice: a meagre wage or unemployment," *Review*, 3 April 1986.

11. National census of 1981, reported in "Are they equal to men in India?" *Economic Times*, 24 October 1982.

12. Figures from Christine Oppong, ILO senior researcher, reported in "An explosion of paid work," *People*, vol. 12, no. 2 (1985).

13. See note 7 above.

14. See note 12 above.

15. Proceedings of Philippines National Population Welfare Congress, reported in "Women still suffer unequal work status in Third World countries," *Business Day* (Manila), 21 December 1981.

16. A study by Gavin Jones of Australian National University, reported in "Employed City Women," *The Bangladesh Observer*, 13 March 1983.

17. Announcement by Bureau of Labor Statistics, U.S. Department of Labor, reported in "Women Gain a Majority in Jobs," *The New York Times*, 19 March 1986.

18. See note 15 above.

19. "The women of Sri Lanka," *Daily News*, 3 July 1982; see note 10 above; "Asia's unions," *Review*, 3 April 1986.

20. "The search for roots reveals a cultural enigma," *Review*, 18 July 1985.

21. Findings of *Yomon* ("women's garden") magazine, reported in "Spate of wife-beating in South Korea," *The Bangladesh Observer*, 23 April 1984.

22. International Planned Parenthood Federation, *Women: progress towards equality* (chart), 1985.

23. "Equality of Malay women—real but restricted," *Review*, 10 April 1986.

24. See note 21 above.

25. "More divorces but the same moral code," *Review*, 19 December 1985.

26. "The women of Sri Lanka" (note 19 above).

27. Address at Philippines National Population Welfare Congress (note 15 above).

## INCHEON, SOUTH KOREA

A portion of this chapter previously appeared in *The Korea Times* (Seoul) in 1984.

1. ILO study, reported in "Third World street traders & odd-jobbers safety valve to unemployment," *Business Recorder*, 27 July 1981.

2. *Ibid.*

3. UNESCO survey cited by Press Foundation of Asia, reported by AFP from Manila, 3 July 1982.

4. ADB, *Project Performance Audit Report, Vocational Training Institutes Project (Korea)*, December 1980.

5. Conducted by the Korea Educational Development Institute.

6. ADB forecasts.

7. ADB figure.

8. "Street vendors problem: Back to square one," *Bangkok World*, 16 November 1984.

## UJUNG PANDANG, INDONESIA

1. Government transmigration figures, reported by Reuters from Jakarta, 23 February 1983; ADB documents; "Transmigration: Indon Version," *The Bangladesh Observer*, 29 November 1983.

2. Statement by then-Transmigration Minister Harun Zain, cited in "Indonesia Begins Relocating People," *The Washington Post*, 11 July 1979.

3. Assessment of World Bank and United Nations agricultural experts, reported in "Jakarta's Push to Move Masses Hits New Snags," *Asian Wall Street Journal*, 7 September 1983.

4. ADB figures and "The 35,000 villages that know growth works," *The Economist* (London), 14 July 1979.

5. Announcement by Transmigration Minister Murtono, reported by AP from Jakarta, 6 March 1984.

## COLOMBO, SRI LANKA

A portion of this chapter previously appeared in the *Far Eastern Economic Review* in 1982.

1. Speech delivered at annual meeting of World Bank and International Monetary Fund, 29 September 1981, in Washington, D.C.

2. ADB, *Agriculture* (see chap. Ashuganj, Bangladesh, note 11).

3. *Ibid.*

4. See, for example, Charles Pearson, *Multinational Corporations, the Environment, and Development* (Washington: World Resources Institute, 1985); proceedings of International Program on Chemical Safety (sponsored by WHO, ILO, and United Nations Environment Program), October 1984, in Nairobi, Kenya; Oxfam studies of pesticide misuse, reported in "22,500 die of pesticides in 3rd World," *Dawn*, 10 December 1984.

5. See, for example, adverse effects of high dams compiled by Environmental Policy Institute, reported in "Actual Price of High Dams Also Includes Social Costs," *The New York Times*, 10 July 1983.

6. "The Third World—Aid and Trade," *The OECD Observer*, November 1981.

7. Statement delivered at annual meeting of World Bank and International Monetary Fund, reported by AFP from Washington, 2 October 1981.

# Index

Peter C. Stuart is a writer and journalist who spent four years in Asia. There he visited most of the region's developing countries, interviewing a cross-section of common people for the Asian Development Bank, an international assistance institution based in Manila. A native of Michigan, he earned bachelor's and master's degrees at the University of Michigan. After working five years at a daily newspaper in his home state, he served 12 years as a staff correspondent of *The Christian Science Monitor*, with postings in New York, Washington, and London, as well as assignments in Latin America and Asia. He has written articles for national magazines and taken part in news broadcasting in the United States and Britain. This is his first book. He and his wife now reside in a village on the banks of the Mississippi River in Illinois.

# THE OTHER HALF

## Glimpses of Grassroots Asia

has been praised by one eminent Asian scholar as "a fine and useful book . . . and significant piece of work" (John Adams, professor of economics, University of Maryland).

To order copies of this book, complete the form below, and mail it with your remittance to:

### F A R    H O R I Z O N    B O O K S

Box 10, Alton, Illinois 62002

-------------------------------------------------------------------------------------

Please send _____ copies of *The Other Half: Glimpses of Grassroots Asia* to:

Name _____

Address _____

City _____ State _____ Zip _____

Price: $9.95 per copy,
plus $1.50 for shipping.

Illinois residents please
add $.60 for sales tax.

Bulk purchase inquiries invited.

Enclosed is a check in the amount of $_____ .